Student Solutions Manual

for use with

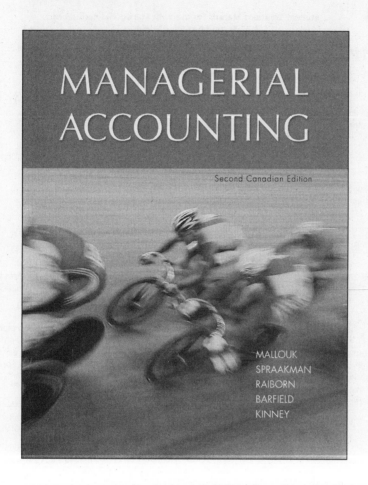

MANAGERIAL
ACCOUNTING

Second Canadian Edition

MALLOUK
SPRAAKMAN
RAIBORN
BARFIELD
KINNEY

Prepared by **BRENDA M. MALLOUK**
UNIVERSITY OF TORONTO

and **GARY SPRAAKMAN**
ATKINSON FACULTY OF LIBERAL AND PROFESSIONAL
STUDIES, YORK UNIVERSITY

THOMSON
NELSON

Australia   Canada   Mexico   Singapore   Spain   United Kingdom   United States

THOMSON

NELSON

**Student Solutions Manual for use with Managerial Accounting,
Second Canadian Edition**

by Brenda M. Mallouk, Gary Spraakman, Cecily A. Raiborn, Jesse T. Barfield, and Michael R. Kinney

Prepared by Brenda M. Mallouk and Gary Spraakman

**Associate Vice President,
Editorial Director:**
Evelyn Veitch

Publisher:
Rod Banister

Senior Marketing Manager:
Charmaine Sherlock

Senior Developmental Editor:
Karina Hope

Senior Production Editor:
Julie van Veen

Senior Production Coordinatior:
Hedy Sellers

Design Director:
Ken Phipps

Cover Design:
Thomson Nelson Media Services

Printer:
Webcom

**Library and Archives Canada
Cataloguing in Publication**

Mallouk, Brenda M.

Student solutions manual for use with Managerial accounting, second Canadian edition / Brenda M. Mallouk, Gary Spraakman.

ISBN 0-17-640728-6

1. Managerial accounting—Problems, exercises, etc.
I. Spraakman, Gary II. Title.

HF5657.4.M348 2005 Suppl. 1
658.15'11   C2005-906702-0

Table of Contents

CHAPTER 1
THE STRATEGIC CONTEXT

QUESTIONS

1. A primary role of information is to reduce the uncertainty that exists in making decisions. In general, the more important the decision, the more crucial the information. Consider, for example, the decision to attend college or university: catalogues are obtained, campus visits are made, financial aid packages are compared, and program requirements are analyzed.

3. This statement is false. Even small companies now have opportunities to arrange partnering with companies in other countries. These opportunities have become available, in part, because of the reduction in tariffs among countries and because of the ability to travel and communicate easily among countries. Also, the reduction in communication costs has increased the opportunities for small companies to operate a global marketplace.

5. Internal information is necessary for managers to plan, control, evaluate performance and make decisions about operations. External information is necessary for managers to evaluate external threats and opportunities and to comply with regulations and laws.

7. Costs could be minimized by simply having no operations, no investment, and no other organizational activities. Hence, costs are a necessary obstacle to generation of revenues. Thus, the objective is not to minimize costs but to maximize the benefits that are derived from cost incurrence.

9. The organizational structure decision is a cost management decision because costs are affected by the organizational structure choice. This chapter discusses two types of organizational structure: centralization and decentralization. Centralization incurs fewer costs but it is less likely to be capable of dealing with production and customer issues. Decentralization incurs more costs but it is more capable of creating additional revenue from dealing more precisely with production and customer issues.

11. Organizational strategy is the link between a firm's goals and objectives and its operational plans. Strategy is therefore a specification of how a firm intends to compete and survive. Each organization will have a unique strategy because it has unique goals, objectives, opportunities, and constraints.

13. Authority is the right, generally because of position or rank, to use resources to accomplish a task or achieve an objective. Responsibility is the obligation to accomplish a task or achieve an objective. Authority can be delegated but responsibility must be assumed and maintained by the person to whom it is assigned. However, responsibility must be accompanied by sufficient authority or the assignment of responsibility cannot endure.

16.   There are two generic strategies: differentiation (adding enough value to charge
       a higher price) and cost leadership (becoming the low-cost producer, and thus
       the low-price seller).

       Differentiation is beneficial because the additional value allows the firm to charge
       a higher price and, hopefully, make a greater return than non-differentiated firms.

       Cost leadership is beneficial because, at least until competitors benchmark the
       organization to learn its 'secrets,' the organization should be able to increase
       volume and generate higher profits. These organizations commonly take full
       advantage of the economics of scale.

18.   Because of the fiduciary nature of not-for-profit organizations, it is essential that
       strategic planning be performed to ensure longevity and fiscal responsibility.
       Thus, it is probably more important (at least legally) for not-for-profit than for-
       profit entities.

20.   The statement is false. Today, many companies have virtually no control over
       prices. Rather, prices are determined by impersonal market forces. Profitability is
       achieved by providing products at the market price and managing costs such that
       the market price exceeds the sum of all costs. Only if a company can somehow
       differentiate its products from its competitors can it attain some control over price.

       Consider, for example, the situation of Internet access. In February 1998, AOL
       announced a $2 increase to its "all-you-can-surf" service fee (up from $19.95 to
       $21.95). Because AOL has about 60% of the U.S. residential subscriber market,
       the fee for all service providers was expected to increase. Part of the need to
       raise fees stemmed from a need to add network capabilities to compete in the
       flat-rate service market--which created a huge increase in AOL's customer base.

22.   Managers must be able to effectively balance short-term and long-term
       considerations in today's business environment because each depends on the
       other to ensure organizational survival. Both are necessary. For example, if an
       organization does not have short-term profitability and continuously innovate to
       keep pace with market demands, it has no chance of long-term survival.
       Alternatively, an organization that plans for the long-term but ignores those
       activities that are necessary in the short-term will also have no chance of long-
       term survival.

25.   The exchange of information within a value creation chain allows each
       participating firm to understand how its actions and costs affect other firms in the
       value creation chain. By exchanging information among firms, components can
       be redesigned, product designs can be improved or simplified, simpler
       distribution channels can be developed, and non-value-adding activities can be
       eliminated. Interorganizational cost management should improve the competitive
       position of an entire value creation chain and make all of its participating firms
       better off.

EXERCISES

Exercise 1
a.   F
b.   F
c.   M
d.   M
e.   F
f.   M
g.   F
h.   M
i.   M
j.   F
k.   M
l.   F
m.   M
n.   M

Exercise 3
a.   2
b.   5
c.   1
d.   4
e.   6
f.   3

Exercise 5
Each student will have a different answer. However, the following items may be mentioned.

a.   Employees might be empowered to decide how long it will take to clean the houses to which they are assigned, how their schedules will be arranged so that all assigned houses are cleaned on time, what activities need to be performed to make the house clean, what equipment and supplies are to be used in the cleaning process, and where (and what) supplies are to be purchased. Employees are in a much better position to judge these issues than an absentee owner. With the input of the employees (as well as approval by you), a standard definition of "clean" that all employees would agree on should be determined.

b.   As the owner, you may retain the billing and supply purchasing processes as well as marketing and customer service. You would also probably want to retain the determination of customer satisfaction through surveys or telephone calls. These matters will be essential to your business profitability and longevity and the employees that you have may not have the expertise or ability (in the form of equipment or knowledge) to engage in these matters.

Exercise 7

a.   The primary benefits of outsourcing the collection function would be to have this function performed by a person or company who could perform the task at a lower cost and more effectively than it could be performed in-house and to eliminate a non-core competency and be able to focus more on jewelry purchasing and sales.

b.   The primary risks of outsourcing the collection function would be that the person or company providing the service is unethical and misrepresents the amount of collections that have been obtained and that the person or company is less concerned about whether all reasonable collection activities have been utilized (because it's not "their" money).

Exercise 9

Each student will have a different answer. No solution is provided.

Exercise 11

a.   The costs of translating from English and reviewing the translation would be the largest costs associated with the additional information. The costs of the additional pages in the annual report would be minimal. The benefits are probably substantial: the translated letter indicates to all readers the high degree of importance that the company places on its international focus and business opportunities. An additional benefit might be that by making the management letter more readable by foreign investors, there could be an increased investment interest.

b.   Each student will have a different answer, but may indicate a need for the company's mission statement, future international acquisition or diversification plans, product development and introduction plans, and utilization of international suppliers within the company's value creation chain.

Exercise 13

Each student will have a different answer. No solution is provided.

CHAPTER 2
COST TERMINOLOGY AND COST FLOWS

QUESTIONS

2. A product cost is incurred to make or acquire inventory or to provide a service. In a manufacturing firm, product costs include direct materials, direct labour, and manufacturing overhead. In a merchandising company, product costs are purchase costs plus freight-in. In a service company, service costs are primarily comprised of direct labour and overhead; direct materials are usually insignificant.

5. This statement is false. Prime cost consists of direct materials cost plus direct labour cost. Conversion cost is composed of the cost of direct labour and overhead. Therefore, the sum of the two would double-count the cost of direct labour and would not equal total product cost.

7. Costs can only be expected to react in a consistent way as long as activity is within the relevant range. That is, only within the relevant range will variable costs remain constant per unit and fixed costs remain constant in total. If the company operates outside of the relevant range, assumptions about cost behaviour are not valid and managers will need to reassess decisions which were based on prior assumptions about cost expectations.

9. A fixed cost remains constant, in total, across changes in the activity measure. A variable cost, in total, varies directly and proportionately with changes in the activity measure.

11. A step cost is a cost that remains constant, in total, across certain intervals of activity. Outside a given activity interval, the total cost changes. A step variable cost remains fixed only for very small activity intervals; a step fixed cost remains constant across wider intervals of activity.

13. This is necessary so that separate variable and fixed predetermined overhead rates can be prepared. If a combined predetermined rate is to be used, there is no need to separate mixed costs for product costing purposes. However, analysis of mixed costs may be done for purposes other than product costing.

16. The four measures are theoretical, practical, normal, and expected capacity. Theoretical capacity assumes production can operate continuously at 100 percent of potential, while practical capacity takes into consideration off-days, downtime, etc., and provides a more attainable measure of output. Normal capacity is the long-run average utilization of the plant's workforce and plant assets; it is customarily about 80 percent of practical capacity. Expected capacity is the anticipated operating level of the company during the next period. Theoretical capacity should be seldom used unless management and stakeholders expect 100 percent plant utilization. It will result in greater underapplication of overhead than the other measures. Practical capacity is a

more realistic measure but is very difficult to attain and will usually result in underapplied overhead. Normal capacity yields a uniform product cost over time and is appealing on that basis. Expected capacity should result in a product cost which approaches actual cost. Any of the capacity levels can result in product costs approaching actual costs if under- or overapplied overhead is allocated to the accounts that contain applied overhead at the end of the year.

18.   The Cost of Goods Manufactured Statement provides an accounting of the material and work in process inventories. The statement shows the beginning balances in each account, what amount of materials were purchased, and what amount of materials were used. The statement also shows the amount of conversion costs incurred during the period and indicates the cost assigned to the goods completed during the period (and transferred to finished goods inventory) and the cost assigned to the ending work in process inventory.

       The statement also presents the flow of production costs for the period: beginning work in process plus production inputs (direct materials + direct labour + manufacturing overhead) minus ending work in process, equals cost of goods manufactured. This sequence of cost flow exactly follows the pattern of production work flow in a manufacturing company.

19.   Least squares regression analysis uses all representative data points (rather than just two) and, therefore, considers much more information than does the high-low method. Least squares define a hypothetically perfect regression line which minimizes the sum of the squares of the differences of actual data points from that regression line. In contrast, the regression line defined by high-low is a simple average line extended between and through the high and low data points. Note that both methods can be used to develop a cost equation.

EXERCISES

Exercise 1

a.	9
b.	13
c	11
d	1
e	4
f	8
g	7
h	None
i	2, 12
j.	10
k.	6
l.	5
m.	3

Exercise 3

a.   Direct material:

Aluminum	$371,000
Wooden ribbing & braces	18,400
	$389,400

b.   Direct labour:

Equipment operators	$120,000

c.   Indirect labour:

Equipment mechanics	$ 54,000
Manufacturing supervisors	28,000
	$ 82,000

Indirect material:

Equipment oil & grease	$ 6,000
Chrome rivets	3,600
	$ 9,600

Exercise 5

a.

Direct materials	$ 718,000
Direct labour	421,000
Total prime cost	$1,139,000

b.

Direct labour		$ 421,000
Overhead:		
Indirect materials	$ 102,000	
Indirect labour	129,000	
Manufacturing utilities	103,000	334,000
Total conversion cost		$755,000

c.   Direct materials $ 718,000

       Direct labour   421,000

       Manufacturing overhead   334,000

       Total cost $1,473,000

Exercise 7

a.   **Component**

         Direct materials:

Wooden cases	$ 4,000
Balls	6,000
Mallets	12,000
Wire hoops	4,800
	$26,800

DM per set: $26,800 ÷ 2,000 sets = $13.40

Manufacturing overhead:

Depreciation	$ 2,400
Supervisor salaries:	4,400
	$6,800

FOH per set: $6,800 ÷ 2,000 sets = $ 3.40

Cost per croquet set:

$13.40 + $3.40 = $16.80

b.   The wooden cases, balls, mallets and wire hoops are expected to be variable. The depreciation and supervisory salaries are expected to be fixed.

c.   By definition, the variable costs would increase because volume is increasing; also, by definition, the fixed costs will remain constant as volume changes.

Total cost for 2,500 sets = $6,800[a] + ($13.40[b] × 2,500)

                        = $6,800 + $33,500

                        = $40,300

[a] $2,400 + $4,400 = $ 6,800

[b] $13.40 Direct materials

Exercise 10

a.   utilities expense = a + bX

       b = ($600 - $150) ÷ ($60,000 - $30,000) = ($450 ÷ $30.000) = $0.015

       a = $600 - ($0.015 × 60,000) = $600 - $900 = $(300)

       Budget formula: Y = $(300) + $0.015 X

b.   The improbable result is the negative fixed cost. Costs cannot be negative unless there is some unusual subsidy involved. The likely reasons for the negative intercept are that one of the data points used was anomalous (an outlier), there is an error in the data, or one of the observations is outside of the relevant range.

Exercise 12

a.

	Repair	Painting
Overhead	$435,000	$965,900
) Activity base:	÷275,600 DL$	÷217,600 MH
Department rate	$1.58 / DL$	$4.44 / MH

Direct materials		$360.00
Direct labour		132.00
Manufacturing overhead (120 x $1.58)	$189.60	
(3 x $4.44)	13.32	202.92
Total costs		$694.92
Desired Profit ($694.92 x 12%)		83.39
Total estimated bill		$778.31

b.
Actual overhead	$442,250.00
Less: Applied overhead (274,920 x $1.58)	434,373.60
Underapplied	$ 7,876.40

Exercise 14

a.   Predetermined Manufacturing Overhead Rate
Estimated manufacturing overhead cost:
Estimated manufacturing overhead cost / Estimated direct labour hours
$360,000 / 144,000 = $2.50 per direct labour hour

b.   Over (under) applied overhead
Manufacturing overhead incurred	$338,000
Manufacturing overhead applied	303,750
Underapplied manufacturing overhead	$(34,250)

c.   Several factors could have caused the above result:
-   Actual production volume, thus direct labour hours, failed to reach the level estimated
-   Labour efficiency proved greater than estimated, causing the base to be smaller relative to incurred overhead, resulting in a higher rate per hour;
-   Manufacturing overhead costs may have been poorly controlled;
-   If there was a mix of products, the mix produced may have been different from that which was estimated, leading to differing OH costs and/or direct labour hours incurred.

Exercise 16

a. $\$72,000 \div 12,000 = \underline{\$6.00}$ per machine hour

b.   Expected capacity = $20,000 \times 0.75 = 15,000$ MH
          Fixed OH rate = $\$72,000 \div 15,000 = \$4.80$ per MH [expected]
          Fixed OH rate   = $\$72,000 \div 20,000 = \$3.60$ per MH [practical]

c.   Total OH rate = $\$6.00 + \$4.80 = \underline{\$10.80}$ [expected]
          Total OH rate = $\$6.00 + \$3.60 = $ $\underline{\$9.60}$ [practical]

          Applied OH = $\$10.80 \times 13,500 = \$145,800$ [expected]
                                     $\$9.60 \times 13,500 = \$129,600$ [practical]

d. $\$145,800 - \$155,000 = \underline{\$(9,200)}$ underapplied
          $\$129,600 - \$155,000 = \underline{\$(25,400)}$ underapplied

e.   Most firms use expected capacity, so their the cost assignments will better approximate actual cost. Use of practical capacity provides better information about efficient utilization of available capacity.

Exercise 18

a.   Applied OH:

Setups	$300 \times \$37 =$	$\$ 11,100
MHs	$9,000 \times \$15 =$	135,000
DLHs	$8,000 \times \$7 =$	56,000
#s rec'd	$100,000 \times \$1 =$	100,000
Returns	$250 \times \$80 =$	20,000
Other	$9,000 \times \$4 =$	36,000
		$\underline{\$358,100}$

b. $\$358,100 - \$362,000 = \underline{\$(3,900)}$ underapplied

c.   Firms are turning to the use of multiple overhead rates to improve cost assignment and cost control. Improvement in these areas is obtained by getting a better relationship between the overhead cost pools and their respective cost drivers. Increasing the number of cost pools increases the homogeneity of the cost pools with regard to their respective cost allocation bases (cost drivers).

Exercise 22

Cost of services rendered
Direct labour:

	Veterinary salaries	$23,000
	Assistant salaries	7,200
	Office salaries	1,700[a]
Total direct labour		$31,900
Supplies		1,400[b]
Overhead:		
Utilities	$ 720	
Depreciation	2,100	
Building rental	1,360[c]	
Total overhead		4,180
Cost of services rendered		$37,480

[a] $3,400 \times 0.50 = \$1,700$
[b] $3,200 - \$1,800 = \$1,400$
[c] $1,700 \times 0.80 = \$1,360$

Exercise 25

i. $33,150   ($14,500 + $59,000 - $12,000 - $28,350)

ii. $75,000   ($60,000 = 80% therefore 100% = $75,000)

iii. $204,000   ($59,700 + $33,150 + $75,000 + $60,000)

iv. $204,000   ($200,000 - $18,000 - $22,000)

v. $110,160   (Number of units sold = $204,000 ÷ $25 = 8,160 units. (All opening inventory sold). X + 15,000 (manufactured in the period) - 8,200 (remaining at the end of the period) = 8,160. X + 6,800 = 8,160 (sold units).

        [X = 1,360 units.] Therefore 1,360 = $17,680 + [(6,800 x $204,000) ÷ 15,000] $92,480 = $110,160

vi. $16,000   ($12,000 + $59,000 - $55,000)

Extract from *Management Accounting Examination*, published by the Certified General Accountants Association of Canada (© CGA-Canada, 1994). Reprinted with permission.

PROBLEMS

Problem 3
a.   Direct materials = $16,900 + $90,000 - $21,700 = $85,200
       Direct labour = 6,800 × $9 = $61,200
       Prime costs = $85,200 + $61,200 = $146,400

b.   Conversion = $61,200 + $109,300 = $170,500

c.   Manufacturing costs:

Direct materials	$ 85,200
Direct labour	61,200
Overhead	109,300
Total manufacturing costs	$255,700
Beginning bal., work in process, 5/1	32,100
Total costs to account for	$287,800
Ending bal., work in process, 5/31	29,600
Cost of goods manufactured	$258,200

d.

Beginning bal., finished goods, 5/1	$ 25,800
Cost of goods manufactured	258,200
Cost of goods available for sale	284,000
Ending bal., finished goods, 5/31	22,600
Cost of goods sold	$261,400

Problem 5
a.

Cost of printing invitations	step fixed
Preparing the theater	step fixed
Postage	variable
Building stage sets	fixed
Printing programs	fixed
Security	fixed
Costumes	fixed

b.   Estimate of attendees = (200 × 0.75) + [2 × (200 × 0.75)]
                            = 150 + (2 × 150) = 450

       Fixed and step fixed costs =
       $260 + $1,000 + $1,215 + $250 + [3 × ($110 + (5 × $30))]= $3,505

       Variable costs = $.30 × 450 = $135
       Total cost = $3,505 + $135 = $3,640

c. $3,640 ÷ 450 = $8.09

d.   Estimate of attendees =
$$(200 \times 0.90) + [2 \times (200 \times 0.90)] = 180 + 360 = \underline{540}$$

Fixed costs and step fixed costs =
$$\$280 + \$1,200 + \$1,215 + \$250 + [3 \times (\$110 + (5 \times \$30))] = \$3,725$$
Total costs = $\$3,725 + (0.30 \times 540) = \underline{\$3,887}$
$\$3,887 \div 540 = \underline{\$7.20}$

Difference due to increase in printing, operating and postage costs.

Problem 8

a. $\dfrac{450 - 150}{900 - 200} = \dfrac{300}{700} = \$0.429 = b$

y = a + \$0.429x
$$\$450 - (\$0.429 \times 900) = \$63.90 = a$$

b.

x	y	xy	x^2	
200	150	30,000	40,000	n = 8
325	220	71,500	105,625	
400	240	96,000	160,000	$\bar{x}$ = 532.5
410	245	100,450	168,100	
525	310	162,750	275,625	$\bar{y}$ = 303.75
680	395	268,600	462,400	
820	420	344,400	672,400	
900	450	405,000	810,000	
4,260	2,430	1,478,700	2,694,150	

$$b = \frac{1,478,700 - (8 \times 532.5 \times 303.75)}{2,694,150 - (8 \times 532.5 \times 532.5)} = \frac{184,725}{425,700} = \$0.434$$

$$a = \$303.75 - (\$0.434 \times 532.5) = \$72.65$$
$$y = \$72.65 + \$0.434x$$

c.   a. y = \$63.90 + (\$0.429 \times 760) = \$389.94
        b. y = \$72.65 + (\$0.434 \times 760) = \$402.49

The answers differ because the high-low method generates slightly different parameters for the cost equation relative to the parameters generated by the least squares method. (It uses all data points.)

d.   The answer to Part b is preferable. This answer is generated by the least squares model which is based on more information than the high-low model.

e.   One concern a manager might have is whether all of the data points are within the relevant range; another concern would be whether any of the observations represent outliers. A manager could also want to know if the cost behaviour from January to August is expected to change, especially when predicting costs into the future.

Problem 12

a.   Increase in RM inventory $ 20,000
      RM used   400,000
      RM purchased $420,000

b.   Increase in WIP $ 60,000
      Cost of Goods Manufactured   800,000
      WIP cost to account for $860,000

      $860,000 - $400,000 = $460,000
      RM used   DL & MOH

      $460,000 = X + 0.60X
      $460,000 = 1.60X
      $287,500 = X = Direct Labour Cost

c.   287,500 × 0.60 = $172,500

d. $200,000 + $800,000 - X = $170,000
      $200,000 + $800,000 - $170,000 = X
      $830,000 = X = COGS

e. $900,000 - $830,000 - $140,000 = $(70,000)

Problem 14

a. $324,000 ÷ $12 = 27,000 sold
      27,000 units sold + 3,000 ending inventory - 0
      Beginning inventory = 30,000 completed

b.   Direct materials issued to production $93,000
      Direct labour   67,000
      Manufacturing insurance   1,800
      Manufacturing utilities   8,100
      Factory depreciation   7,900
            $177,800

      $177,800 - $18,000 ending work in process = $159,800

c. $159,800 ÷ 30,000 = $5.33 cost per unit of goods manufactured

d.   Raw materials inventory   124,000
               Accounts payable   124,000
       To record cost of direct
       materials purchased on account

       Work in process inventory   93,000
               Raw materials inventory   93,000
       To record direct materials
       transferred to production

       Work in process inventory   67,000
               Salaries and wages payable   67,000
       To record wages

       Fixed overhead   1,800
               Prepaid insurance   1,800
       To record expired insurance

       Fixed or variable overhead   8,100
               Utilities payable   8,100
       To record fixed utility cost

       Fixed overhead   7,900
               Accumulated depreciation   7,900
       To record depreciation

       Work in process inventory   17,800
               Fixed or variable overhead   17,800
       Transfer overhead costs

       Finished goods inventory   159,800
               Work in process inventory   159,800
       To record work completed

       Accounts receivable   324,000
               Sales   324,000
       To record sales

       Cost of goods sold   *   143,910
               Finished goods   143,910
       To record cost of goods sold.
       * (27,000 units @ $5.33)

Problem 16

	Case #1	Case #2	Case #3
Sales	$9,300	19,700[k]	$112,000
Direct materials used	1,200	6,100[h]	18,200
Direct labour	2,500[a]	4,900	32,100[m]
Prime cost	3,700	11,000[i]	50,300[n]
Conversion cost	4,800	8,200	49,300
Overhead	2,300[b]	3,300[g]	17,200
Cost of goods manufactured	6,200	14,000	68,900[o]
Beg. work in process	500	900	5,600
Ending work in process	300[c]	1,200	4,200
Beginning finished goods	800[e]	1,900	7,600
Ending finished goods	1,200	3,700[l]	4,300[p]
Cost of goods sold	5,800[d]	12,200	72,200
Gross profit	3,500	7,500[j]	39,800[q]
Operating expenses	1,300[f]	3,500	18,000
Net income (loss)	2,200	4,000	21,800[r]

[a] $3,700 - 1,200 = 2,500$

[b] $4,800 - 2,500 = 2,300$

[c] $500 + 1,200 + 2,500 + 2,300 - 6,200 = 300$

[d] $9,300 - 3,500 = 5,800$

[e] $5,800 - 6,200 + 1,200 = 800$

[f] $3,500 - 2,200 = 1,300$

[g] $8,200 - 4,900 = 3,300$

[h] $14,000 + 1,200 - 900 - 8,200 = 6,100$

[i] $6,100 + 4,900 = 11,000$

[j] $4,000 + 3,500 = 7,500$

[k] $12,200 + 7,500 = 19,700$

[l] $1,900 + 14,000 - 12,200 = 3,700$

[m] $49,300 - 17,200 = 32,100$

[n] $18,200 + 32,100 = 50,300$

[o] $18,200 + 32,100 + 17,200 + 5,600 - 4,200 = 68,900$

[p] $7,600 + 68,900 - 72,200 = 4,300$

[q] $112,000 - 72,200 = 39,800$

[r] $39,800 - 18,000 = 21,800$

CHAPTER 3
COST–VOLUME–PROFIT ANALYSIS

QUESTIONS

1. The breakeven point is a point of reference by which a manager can gauge risk. The more that sales exceed the breakeven point, the smaller is the risk of not being profitable or of suffering a loss if a downturn in business occurs.

3. Breakeven analysis uses the same model as CVP except that the P [or profit term] is set to zero and therefore ignored.

5. Answers may vary, but all the assumptions have a tendency to reduce the model's realism. As realism is reduced, so is the ability of the model to predict actual results. The quantities indicated by CVP analysis should be taken as approximately correct and not be considered as absolutes.

7. Tony Soprano, the company president, should be concerned. A slight reduction in volume could possibly produce losses for the company. He needs to make sure volume stays up.

9. CVP renders a short-run perspective because the assumptions that underlie CVP are true only in the short run. The implications of this are that managers should expect the results from CVP analysis to hold only temporarily and should also integrate longer run considerations into their problem-solving analyses for a balanced perspective.

12. The "bag" assumption means that a multi-product firm will consider that the products it sells are sold in a constant, proportional sales mix--as if in a bag of goods. It is necessary to make this assumption in order to determine the contribution margin for the entire company product line since individual product contribution margins may differ significantly. Since a single contribution margin must be used in CVP analysis, the "bag" assumption allows CVP computations to be made.

14. Some fixed costs can be traced directly to a product line, but the discontinuation of the product line may not result in termination of the cost. Examples of such costs would include the salaries of managers who could not be dismissed if the product line were terminated, and the depreciation charges associated with production equipment for which there is no alternative use.

16.
Cost of goods sold	B
Contribution margin	V
Gross Margin	A
Selling expenses	B
Variable expenses	V
Administrative expenses	B
Fixed expenses	V

18.   Absorption and variable costing each recognize the following as product costs: direct materials, direct labour, and variable manufacturing overhead. Additionally, absorption costing recognizes fixed manufacturing overhead as a product cost. Both costing approaches treat selling and administrative costs as period costs.

20.   Absorption costing recognizes fixed manufacturing overhead as a product cost. Accordingly, under absorption costing, fixed overhead flows through the inventory accounts and is eventually expensed through the cost of goods sold. Alternatively, variable costing treats fixed manufacturing overhead as a period cost and it is deducted in its entirety in the period in which it is incurred.

    This is important because under Variable Costing the fixed manufacturing overhead is expensed in the period in which it is incurred. Writing off fixed overhead in the period in which it is incurred is best for performance evaluation because it does not allow management to hide fixed costs in ending inventory to increase profits.

EXERCISES

Exercise 1
BEP in units = $400,000 ÷ ($15 - $11) = <u>100,000</u> units;
BEP in dollars = 100,000 units X $15 = $1,500,000

Exercise 3
SP is used to designate selling price.
10,000 X (SP - 0.60 SP) - $40,000 = $10,000
10,000 X (0.40 SP) = $50,000
4,000 SP = $50,000
SP = <u>$12.50</u>

Exercise 5
a.   Units sales = ($80,000 + $40,000)) $5 = <u>24,000</u> units
      24,000 X $8 = <u>$192,000</u>

b.   Profit before taxes = $25,000) 0.6 = $41,667
      Unit sales = ($41,667 + $40,000) ÷ $4 = <u>20,417</u> units
      20,417 X ($6 + $4) = <u>$204,170</u>

c.   Profit before taxes = $54,000 ÷ 0.6 = $90,000
      Unit sales = ($90,000 + $60,000) ÷ ($10 X 0.3) = <u>50,000</u> units
      50,000 X $10 = <u>$500,000</u>

d.   Profit before taxes = $30,000 ÷ 0.50 = $60,000
      Unit sales = ($60,000 + $60,000) ÷ $3 = <u>40,000</u>
      40,000 X ($3 ÷ (1 - 0.7)) = <u>$400,000</u>

e.   Profit before taxes = $40,000 ÷ 0.5 = $80,000
      Unit sales = ($80,000 + $25,000) ÷ (0.25 ($9 ÷ 0.75)) = <u>35,000</u> units
      35,000 X ($9 ÷ 0.75) = <u>$420,000</u>

Exercise 7
a. BEP = $16,200 ÷ ($10.00 - $4.60)
       = $16,200 ÷ $5.40 = <u>3,000</u> books

    Profit before taxes = (Volume X CM) - FC
                       = [(3,200 X $5.40) - $16,200] = <u>$1,080</u>

b. BEP = $21,600 ÷ $5.40 = 4,000 books
    Profit before taxes = [(5,200 X $5.40) - $21,600]
                         = <u>$6,480</u>

Exercise 9
a.

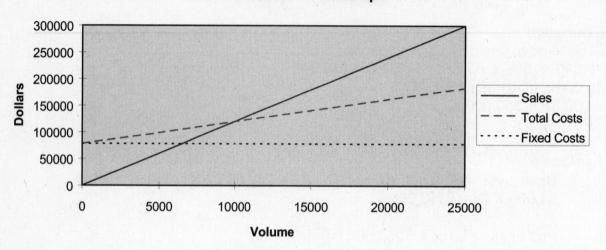

b.

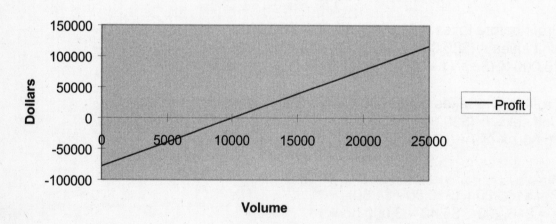

Exercise 11
a.

	Compact Carts	Standard Carts	Bag*
Sales	$2,000	$3,500	$9,000
Variable costs	1,800	3,000	7,800
CM	$ 200	$ 500	$1,200

*Each bag has 1 compact and 2 standard carts.

    BEP = $360,000,000) $1,200 = 300,000 bags
    Compact carts = 300,000 X 1 = <u>300,000</u>
    Standard carts = 300,000 X 2 = <u>600,000</u>

b.

	Compact	Standard	Bag*
Sales	$2,000	$3,500	$5,500
Variable costs	1,800	3,000	4,800
CM	$ 200	$ 500	$ 700

*Each bag contains one compact and one standard cart.

BEP = $360,000,000 ÷ $700 = 514,286 bags (rounded)
Compact carts = 514,286 X 1 = <u>514,286</u>
Standard carts = 514,286 X 1 = <u>514,286</u>

In Part a, only 900,000 total carts had to be sold to break even. In Part b, a total of 1,028,572 carts must be sold to break even. The difference is caused by a shift in the sales mix requiring more of the lower (per unit) profit carts to be sold relative to the higher profit carts.

c.

	Compact Cart	Standard Cart	Bag*
Sales	$2,000	$3,500	$13,000
Variable costs	1,800	3,000	11,400
CM	$ 200	$ 500	$ 1,600

*Each bag contains 60% or 3 compact carts and 40% or 2 standard carts.

    BEP = $425,000,000 ÷ 1,600 = 265,625 bags
    Compact carts = 265,625 X 3 = <u>796,875</u>
    Standard carts = 265,625 X 2 = <u>531,250</u>

Exercise 13

a.   Total cost, manual line = (100,000 x $7) + $150,000   = <u>$850,000</u>

Total cost, automated line = (100,000 x $3) + $630,000   = <u>$930,000</u>

The manual line would be most cost effective.

Manual line, BEP = $150,000) $3   = <u>50,000</u> units
Automated line, BEP = $630,000) $7   = <u>90,000</u> units

MOS, manual line = (100,000 - 50,000) x $10   = <u>$500,000</u>
MOS, automated line = (100,000 - 90,000) x $10 = <u>$100,000</u>

b.   Total cost, manual line = (120,000 x $7) + $150,000   = <u>$990,000</u>

Total cost, automated line = (120,000 x $3) + $630,000= <u>$990,000</u>
One would be indifferent between the two lines

c.   Total cost, manual line = (150,000 x $7) + $150,000   = <u>$1,200,000</u>

Total cost, automated line = (150,000 x $3) + $630,000= <u>$1,080,000</u>
Yes, now the automated line would be preferred.

d.   Income before taxes = $60,000 ÷ (1-0.4)   = $100,000
Manual line:
To cover fixed and variable costs and provide $100,000 income before tax, total
sales must = ($7 x 100,000) + $150,000 + $100,000 = <u>$950,000</u>
Unit sales price = $950,000 ÷ 100,000 = <u>$9.50</u>

Automated line: (see above)
Total sales = ($3 x 100,000) + $630,000) + $100,000 = <u>$1,030,000</u>

Unit sales price   = <u>$10.30</u>

Exercise 15
Absorption costing:

Ending inventory
Ending inventory
Direct Material [($600,000 ÷ 200,000) x 25,000]   = $ 75,000
Direct labour [($450,000 ÷ 200,000) x 25,000]   =   56,250
Manufacturing Overhead [($600,000 ÷ 200,000) x 25,000]   =   75,000
                                                               $206,250

or ($600,000 + $450,000 + $600,000) X (25,000 ÷ 200,000) = <u>$206,250</u>

Variable costing:
  Total labour hours = $450,000 ÷ $10 = <u>45,000</u>
  Fixed overhead = 45,000 X $6 = <u>$270,000</u>
  Variable overhead = $600,000 - $270,000 = <u>$330,000</u>

Ending inventory
      = ($600,000 + $450,000 + $330,000) X (25,000 ÷ 200,000) = <u>$172,500</u>

Exercise 17

a.   Total CGS ($109,250 − $54,625) $ 54,625
       Variable product cost (9,500 x $3.50)   33,250
       Fixed production costs in CGS $ 21,375

       Fixed production cost per unit: $21,375 ÷ 9,500 = $2.25
       Total production = $22,500 ÷ $2.25 = <u>10,000</u> units

b.   Sales $109,250
       Cost of goods sold ($109,250 − $54,625)   54,625
       Gross margin (profit) $ 54,625
       Selling and administrative expenses   38,000
       Profit before taxes $ 16,625

PROBLEMS

Problem 1

a.   BEP in rings = $\dfrac{\$42,000 + \$56,000 + 30,000}{\$250 - (\$90 + \$18 + \$8)}$ = <u>955</u> units

       BEP in revenue = 955 units X $250 selling price = $238,750

b.   Revenue = $\dfrac{\$128,000 + \$140,000}{(134 \div 250)}$ = <u>$500,000</u>

c.   Profit before tax = $120,000 ÷ 0.7 = $171,429

       Required revenue = $\dfrac{(128,000 + \$171,429)}{(134 \div 250)}$ = <u>$558,636</u>

d.   R = (128,000 + 0.2857R) ÷ 0.536 = <u>$511,386.33</u>

e.   Current profit:

CM (2,200 rings x $134)	$294,800
Less fixed cost	128,000
Profit before tax	$166,800
Less tax ($166,800 x 0.30)	50,040
Net profit	$116,760

Alternative:	
[(1.25 x 2,200) x ($134 – $20)]	$313,500
Less fixed cost ($128,000 + $12,000)	140,000
Profit before tax	$173,500
Less tax ($173,500 x 0.30)	52,050
Net profit	$121,450

       The alternative appears to be preferred based on the quantitative measure.
       Before making a decision qualitative factors should also be considered.

Problem 4

a.   At a fare of $2,000 Onexa Air could expect to have 190 business travellers and
       20 pleasure travellers

Variable costs per passenger:	
Food and beverages	$ 40
Ticket commissions @ 8% of fare	160
	$200

Contribution margin per passenger would be would be $2,000 - $200 = $1,800

Contribution margin from business travellers:

At $500:	$420 x 200 =	$ 84,000
At $2,000	$1,800 x 190 =	$342,000

Contribution margin from pleasure travellers:

At $500	$420 x 100 =	$ 42,000
At $2,000	$1,800 x 20 =	$ 36,000

b. The key factor which affects this analysis is the relative elasticity of demand of the two-classes of travellers. Business travellers' demand is relatively price inelastic because often they must get to their destination and back to their office as expediently as possible, and their fare is usually paid by their employers. A 300% increase in fares will result in only a 5% reduction in business travellers. By contrast, pleasure travellers often have much greater flexibility in when they travel to and from their destination. A potential saving of $1,500 (which is usually "out of their own pocket") is a strong incentive to time their travel plans so as to satisfy any restrictive requirement. Put another way, their demand is highly price elastic--a 300% increase in fares would result in an 80% drop in pleasure travellers. There are also several factors that should be taken into consideration when deciding what fare(s) to charge. For instance, the cost of food and beverages is variable on a per passenger basis--it does not vary in relation to revenue. Therefore, other things being equal, the contribution margin from the $2,000 fare is preferable. Also, while the commission does vary in direct proportion to the fare revenue, it is a low rate (8%) and does not have much impact--the $2,000 fare is still preferable.

c. Since Onexa-Air generates sits maximum contribution at a combination of different round-trip fares for business and pleasure travellers, it would be in the company's best interest to create a differential fare structure. Clearly, Onexa-Air could not asks travellers which reason they have for travelling, as everyone would answer "pleasure" if it meant a $1,500 reduction in fare. However, an effective way to achieve the same result would be to require that to qualify for the $500 fare, the traveller would have to stay over a Saturday night.

Problem 6
a   i. Calculation of minimum price

Total overhead = $1,500,000, which is 25% of direct labour costs
    Variable overhead:
        ($1,500,000 – $900,000) ÷ $1,500,000 x 100% = 40% of total overhead or
    Variable Overhead rate is 25% x 40% = 10% of direct labour cost

Total variable costs of production on quoted boat:

Direct material	$ 50,000
Direct labour	80,000
Variable overhead @ 10% of direct labour [1]	8,000
Total variable costs of production	$138,000

[1] 40% of $20,000

The minimum price Mr. Spraakman, Senior could quote without increasing or decreasing company net income is $138,000. This is because at this price, the selling price would equal variable costs and contribution margin would be $0.

ii.
Customer's offer	$150,000
Variable costs of production	138,000
Contribution to profit	$ 12,000

In accepting the customer's offer, the company increases net income by $12,000 for the year.

b.   The contribution approach allows the decision maker to focus on whether the additional revenue generated by the sale of the products will cover the additional cost required to produce them, and whether there will be anything "left over" to contribute towards fixed costs and/or profit. If the incremental revenue exceeds the incremental cots, and if there is excess capacity, in the short run, it is economically beneficial to accept the order, even if it does not cover "full" costs.

A major disadvantage of the contribution approach is its short-run focus. In the long run, a company must sell its products at a price sufficient to cover its total costs, including fixed costs. If it cannot obtain a price in excess of its full costs of production, the company will not remain economically viable.

Problem 10

a.

	Laptop	Standard	Luxury	Bag
Sales	$2,200	$ 3,700	$6,000	$ 37,100
Variable costs	1,900	3,000	5,000	30,700
CM	$ 300	$ 700	$1,000	$ 6,400

BEP = $1,080,000,000 ÷ $6,400   = 168,750 bags
Laptop computers = 168,750 x 3   = 506,250
Standard computers = 168,750 x 5   = 843,750
Luxury computers = 168,750 x 2   = 337,500

b.   Unit volume (bags)
= (($1,000,000,000 ÷ 0.5) + $1,080,000,000) ÷ $6,400 = <u>481,250</u> bags

Laptop computers = 481,250 x 3   = <u>1,443,750</u>
Standard computers = 481,250 x 5   = <u>2,406,250</u>
Luxury computers = 481,250 x 2   = <u>962,500</u>

c.

	Laptop	Standard	Luxury	Bag
Sales	$2,200	$3,700	$6,000	$ 31,800
Variable costs	1,900	3,000	5,000	26,500
CM	$ 300	$ 700	$1,000	$ 5,300

Unit volume (bags)

= (($1,000,000,000) 0.5) + $1,080,000,000) ÷ $5,300 = 581,132 bags

Laptop computers = 581,132 x 5   = <u>2,905,660</u>
Standard computers = 581,132 x 4   = <u>2,324,528</u>
Luxury computers = 581,132 x 1   = <u>581,132</u>

d.   On a unit-for-unit basis, luxury computers generate more contribution margin than the other models. Accordingly, as the mix shifts to more luxury computers, the BEP (in units) will drop and the number of computers to be sold to reach a specified profit goal will drop.

Problem 12
a.   Total revenue per bag $24
Total variable cost per bag   12
Contribution margin per bag $12

CM% for a bag ($12) $24)   <u>50%</u>

b.   BEP = $12,000 ÷ 0.50 = $24,000
$24,000 ÷ $24 = 1,000 bags
Ducks = 1,000 x 1 = 1,000
Ducklings = 1,000 x 2 = 2,000

Ducks dollar sales = 1,000 x $12 = $ 12,000
Ducklings dollar sales = 2,000 x $6 =   12,000
Total $ 24,000

c.   Revenue = ($12,000 + $24,000) ÷ 0.50 = $72,000
$72,000 ÷ $24 = 3,000 sets
Ducks = 3,000 x 1 = <u>3,000</u>
Ducklings = 3,000 x 2 = <u>6,000</u>

d.   Total revenue per bag $42
            Total variable cost per bag   24
            Contribution margin per bag $18

            CM% for a bag ($18 ÷ $42) = 0.4286
            Profit before tax = $9,000 ÷ (1 - 0.40) = $15,000
            Revenue = ($15,000 + $12,000) ÷ 0.4286 = $63,000   (rounded)
            $63,000 ÷ $42 = 1,500 sets
            Ducks = 1,500 x 1 = 1,500
            Ducklings = 1,500 x 5 = 7,500

Problem 14

a.   Based on quantitative facts only the sales manager would be advised to
            accept the order. His calculations for decision making are incorrect. The
            following contribution per unit should be used in the analysis.

            Special order sales price $ 26.00
            Cost of goods sold ($1,006,400 ÷ 50,000) $20.128
            Marketing and administrative   0*   20.128
            Contribution margin $ 5.872
            Add: Savings on labels   0.300
            Net contribution per unit $ 6.172

The order will contribute to the company's net income before taxes $61,720
(10,000 x $6.172).

*This extra contribution excludes marketing and administrative expenses, which
as stated in the problem will not be incurred for this order.

b.   i.   Break-even   =   Fixed Costs) Unit sales price - Unit variable cost
                           =   ($323,600[1] + $104,000[2]) ÷ ($37[3] - $23.048)
                           = $427,600 ÷ $13.952
                           =   30,648 clubs

            [1]   Fixed cost of goods sold = $1,330,000 - $1,006,400
            [2]   Marketing and Administration = $250,000 - $146,000
            [3]   Sales price per club $1,850,000 ÷ 50,000

      ii.   The company has a margin of safety of 50,000 - 30,648 units or 38.7%

Problem 16

a.

	VPI		Tech	
Profit before taxes	$20,000	$38,000	$20,000	$48,000
Tax expenses	8,000	15,200	8,000	19,200
Fixed costs	10,000	10,000	50,000	50,000
Variable costs	70,000	112,000	30,000	42,000
Total CM	30,000	48,000	70,000	98,000
CM ratio	0.30	0.30	0.70	0.70

BEP = Fixed costs) CM ratio

VPI - breakeven = $10,000 ÷ 0.30 = $33,333

Tech-breakeven = $50,000 ÷ 0.70 = $71,429

b.

CM	$ 30,000	$ 48,000	$ 70,000	$ 98,000
Divide by PBT	$ 20,000	$ 38,000	$ 20,000	$ 48,000
DOL =	1.5	1.26	3.5	2.04

c.   Desired profit after-tax = $200,000 x 0.12 = $24,000

Profit before tax = $24,000 ÷ 0.60 = $40,000

VPI: (Sales x 0.30) – $10,000 = $40,000

Sales x 0.30 = $50,000

Sales = $166,667

Tech: (Sales x 0.70) - $50,000 = $40,000

Sales x 0.70 = $90,000

Sales = $128,571

d.   VPI's cost structure consists of a greater proportion of variable costs and a smaller proportion of fixed costs then Tech. In a slow market, or at low volume levels, this cost structure will generate larger profits or smaller losses that Tech's cost structure. Proof of this is found in comparing the two firm's breakeven points. Alternatively, Tech's cost structure is favoured when volume turns up because less of each dollar goes to cover variable costs. The value of this cost structure is demonstrated in the answers to part c. Thus, the cost structure of VPI is less risky; but the cost structure of Tech offers more upside potential.

Problem 21
Absorption Costing

	Year 1	Year 2	Year 3	Year 4
Sales	$3,300,000	$4,510,000	$4,620,000	$4,950,000
CGS:				
BWIP	0	456,000	380,000	380,000
CGM	2,736,000	3,040,000	3,192,000	3,040,000
Available	2,736,000	$3,496,000	3,572,000	3,420,000
EWIP	456,000	380,000	380,000	0
	$2,280,000	$3,116,000	$3,192,000	$3,420,000
VV	20,000	0	(10,000)	0
CGS adj.	$2,300,000	$3,116,000	$3,182,000	3,420,000
GM	$1,000,000	$1,394,000	$1,438,000	$1,530,000
Op Exp.	380,000	446,000	452,000	470,000
NIBT	$ 620,000	$948,000	$986,000	$1,060,000

Variable Costing

	Year 1	Year 2	Year 3	Year 4
Sales	$3,300,000	$4,510,000	$ 4,620,000	$4,950,000
CGS				
BWIP	0	426,000	355,000	355,000
CGM	2,556,000	2,840,000	2,982,000	2,840,000
Available for Sale	$2,556,000	$3,266,000	$ 3,337,000	$3,195,000
Less: EWIP	(426,000)	(355,000)	(355,000)	0
	2,130,000	$2,911,000	$ 2,982,000	$3,195,000
Product CM	$1,170,000	$1,599,000	$ 1,638,000	$1,755,000
Less: Var. Sell.	(180,000)	(246,000)	(252,000)	(270,000)
Total CM	$ 990,000	$1,353,000	$ 1,386,000	$1,485,000
Less: Fixed Cost	(400,000)	(400,000)	(400,000)	(400,000)
NIBT	$ 590,000	$ 953,000	$ 986,000	$1,085,000

Problem 23

<u>2006</u>

Fixed OH rate = $50,000 ÷ 5,000 = $10 per unit

OH put in inventory = $10 x (5,000 - 4,000) = $10,000

VC income = $80,000 - $10,000 = <u>$70,000</u>

<u>2007</u>

Fixed OH rate = $54,000 ÷ 6,000 = $9

OH in units placed in inventory = 2,000 x $9 =	$18,000
OH in units taken from inventory = 1,000 x 10 =	<u>10,000</u>
Net addition to inventory	<u>$ 8,000</u>

VC income = $110,000 - $8,000 = <u>$102,000</u>

<u>2008</u>

Fixed overhead rate = $70,000 ÷ 7,000 = $10

OH in units placed in inventory = $10 x 2,000 =	$20,000
OH in units taken from inventory = $9 x 2,000 =	<u>18,000</u>
Net addition to inventory	<u>$ 2,000</u>

VC income = $200,000 - $2,000 = <u>$198,000</u>

Problem 24

a.   Sales price = product CM + DM + DL + Variable OH

        = $8 + $3 + $5 + $2

        = <u>$18</u>

b.   Total contribution margin = $200,000 + $200,000 + $350,000 = <u>$750,000</u>

        Unit total contribution margin = $18 - ($3 + $5 + $2 + $2) = <u>$6</u>

        Units sold = $750,000) $6 = 125,000 units

        Total sales = $18 x 125,000 = <u>$2,250,000</u>

c.   Units sold = <u>125,000</u> (as calculated in b)

d.

Reed Incorporated

Variable Cost Income Statement

for the year ended 2008

Sales (125,000 x $18)		$2,250,000
Less: Variable CGS ($10 x 125,000)		1,250,000
Product contribution margin		$1,000,000
Less: Variable S&A expenses ($2 x 125,000)		250,000
Total contribution margin		$ 750,000
Less fixed expenses:		
Manufacturing overhead	$200,000	
S&A	350,000	550,000
Net income		$ 200,000

Problem 25

MJ Company

Income Statement

Year ended December 31, 2008

Sales			$5,000,000
Cost of goods sold			
Variable (300,000 @ $10)		$3,000,000	
Fixed		4,000,000	
Available for sale		$7,000,000	
Less: Ending Inventory			
Variable (200,000 @ $10)	$2,000,000		
Fixed (2/3 x 4,000,000)	2,666,667	4,666,667	2,333,333
Gross Profit			$2,666,667
Less: General and administrative expense			500,000
Income before President's bonus			$2,166,667
Less: President's bonus			1,083,334
Income before taxes			$1,083,333

b.   The income statement for 2008 (as well as 2007) is based on the absorption
      costing method. As we can see in part a under this costing method $2,666,667 of
      fixed costs have been deferred in inventory. The President has not been able to

increase the sales nor reduce the costs from 2008. She has not really improved the company's performance from the previous year so it is debatable as to why she should be entitled to such a large bonus.

c. Under variable costing, the net loss in 2007 would be the same as shown in the absorption costing income statement, that is, a loss of $500,000. There was no change in inventories, hence, all fixed costs were expensed in 2007 under absorption costing.

In 2008, under variable costing, the net loss before the President's bonus would be $500,000 since none of the fixed overhead costs would be deferred in ending inventory. Instead the $2,666,667 that was deferred under absorption costing would be expensed in 2007 under variable costing.

d. The President would be indifferent to the product costing approach used at the sales level where units produced equal units sold. Assuming that the President would want to use absorption costing and produce more than the units sold, the constraint would become the maximum plant capacity of 400,000 units. If the market increases such that sales increase to 400,000 units, both costing methods will produce the same result. At this level it will be impossible to build up

ending inventory and therefore, impossible to bury any of the period's fixed costs in ending inventory. Consequently she will not be able to keep some of the period's fixed costs off the income statement for the period.

e. The President would prefer variable costing where the sales level is greater than production. This is because under absorption costing not only the current period's fixed manufacturing costs are expensed against sales but also the portion of the prior period's fixed manufacturing costs which were inventoried in the last period and sold in this period.

CHAPTER 4
COSTING SYSTEMS

QUESTIONS

2. More than anything else, a machine-paced production system needs a product costing system that adequately considers the factors that generate product costs. In a labour-paced environment, overhead is probably labour-driven. In a machine-paced environment, most of the overhead costs will be machine related. Thus, the application of overhead rate should be based on machine usage. To properly control and track machine costs, some firms have even resorted to the use of a fourth cost pool, machine costs, in addition to the traditional cost pools of direct materials, direct labour, and overhead.

4. Job order costing and process costing are similar in that they are both methods of assigning costs to products and each uses an averaging technique. Both methods also use similar product accounts (Raw Material Inventory, Work in Process Inventory, Finished Goods Inventory, Cost of Goods Sold) to capture the costs associated with production and use similar cost pools (DM, DL, OH). Costs are accumulated by department under each system and costs follow the related products through the entire manufacturing process.

    Job order and process costing differ in the determination of the goods to which to assign departmental costs. In a job order system, departmental costs are assigned only to the job for which those costs were incurred. In a process costing system, departmental costs are assigned to all products (assuming that they are all alike) that flow through that department. Job order costing does not have a need for the use of equivalent units of production, which is essential to process costing.

6. Equivalent units of production (EUP) is used in process costing to approximate the number of whole units of output that could have been produced during a period from the actual effort expended during that period. Equivalent units of production allow partially and fully completed units to be accounted for on a comparable basis. Without use of EUP, partially and fully completed units would be combined as if they were homogeneous measures of output--resulting in meaningless data. Job order costing assigns specific departmental costs directly to the related jobs based on the degree of completion of that job.

7. The six steps follow:

    a. Calculate the total number of physical units to account for.
    b. Calculate the total number of physical units that have been accounted for in units transferred out and units in ending work in process.
    c. Compute equivalent units of production for each cost component.
    d. Determine the total cost to account for, which equals beginning inventory cost plus current period cost.

e.   Calculate the cost per equivalent unit for each cost component.
f.   Assign the costs per equivalent unit to the goods transferred out and to
        the goods remaining in ending inventory.

9.   Units "started and completed" in a period are calculated as total units completed
        during the period minus units in the beginning inventory. This figure can be used
        in both the weighted average and FIFO methods, as shown in the computations
        in the chapter. (There are, however, other methods of computing weighted
        average EUP in which the units started and completed are not shown
        separately.) This calculation is not essential for the weighted average method
        because work performed on the current period's beginning inventory in the prior
        period need not be separated from work performed to complete the beginning
        inventory in the current period. This calculation is essential for the FIFO method
        because work in the prior period cannot be commingled with work performed in
        the current period.

10.   The cost of production report is prepared for each department or each process.
        This document accounts for both the costs and the units in a department's
        beginning inventory as well as the current period costs and units. Per-unit costs
        are developed using equivalent units of production. These per-unit costs are then
        used to determine the cost of the goods that have been transferred out to either a
        successor WIP department or to Finished Goods Inventory and the cost of the
        goods in ending WIP.

12.   The cost per unit transferred out will always be equal to the cost per unit
        transferred in if the two sequential departments do not change the unit of
        measure. If, however, the two sequential departments change from (for example)
        litres of output to fifty-litre cans of input, the cost per unit of measure will need to
        be adjusted. The total cost transferred in will, however, always be the same
        regardless of whether there is a shift in the unit of measure.

13.   The journal entry would be the one that recognizes the transfer of goods from the
        most downstream department to finished goods: a debit to Finished Goods
        Inventory and a credit to Work in Process--Finishing.

18.   Spoilage creates an important cost of quality. As such, spoilage costs should be
        monitored so that a formal evaluation can be made of efforts to control spoilage
        costs. If not specifically tracked, spoilage costs are merely averaged over the
        good units produced. In tracking spoilage costs, some firms may want to
        distinguish between expected (or normal) spoilage and unexpected (abnormal)
        spoilage. World-class companies, however, would generally utilize a zero defects
        concept that would classify all spoilage as abnormal.

20.   The cost of spoilage is difficult to determine for a service provider because
        spoilage is often defined as "poor service." If a customer does not complain and
        simply does not return to use the services of the provider again, there is no way
        to determine the cost impact on the company.

EXERCISES

Exercise 1

a = $12,000 X 0.80 = $9,600
b = $10,000 ÷ 0.80 = $12,500
c + d = $27,400 - $9,400 = $18,000 and d = 0.80 c
Therefore: c + 0.80 c = $18,000
Thus c = $10,000
d = $10,000 X 0.80 = $8,000
e = $5,000 + $12,000 + $9,600 = $26,600
f = $7,000 + $12,500 + $10,000 = $29,500

Exercise 3

Raw Materials Inventory	80,000	
Accounts Payable		80,000
Work in Process	38,000	
Raw Materials Inventory		38,000
Manufacturing Overhead	2,000	
Raw Materials Inventory		2,000

Exercise10

a. Total direct material cost is $234,000; the total tonnes of material consumed
    would be $234,000) $50 = 4,680. Therefore, the overhead rate is
    $439,920) 4,680 = $94 per tonne.

b.
Bridge 1:	($45,000 ÷ $50) x $94	$ 84,600
Bridge 2:	($54,000 ÷ $50) x $94	101,520
Bridge 3:	($135,000 ÷ $50) x $94	253,800
Total overhead		$439,920

c.
	Bridge 1	Bridge 2	Bridge 3
Direct materials	$ 45,000	$ 54,000	$135,000
Direct labour	180,000	213,000	599,000
Overhead	84,600	101,520	253,800
Total	$309,600	$368,520	$987,800

d. The year-ending WIP = $309,600 + $368,520 = $678,120.

Exercise 12

a. i)   Direct Materials Used:

$54,000 + $219,000 - $39,000 = $234,000

$234,000 x 90% = $210,600

ii)   Work-In-Process on December 31, 2008

$15,000 + $60,000 + (7,500 x $4.50) = $108,750

iii)   Cost of Goods Manufactured in 2008

$82,500 + $210,600 + $264,000 + (33,000 x $4.50) - $108,750 = $596,850

iv)   Finished Goods Inventory on December 31, 2008

$90,000 + $596,850 - ($744,000 x 75%) = $128,850

v)   Actual Manufacturing Overhead incurred in 2008

33,000 DLHRS x $4.50 per DLHR + $750 = $149,250

b. If the amount is immaterial the entire over/underapplied overhead amount is closed to cost of goods sold. If the amount is material the under/over applied overhead is closed to cost of goods sold, finished goods inventory and work-in-process inventory in the ratio of their individual balances to the total of the three combined.

Exercise 14

a.	Total litres to account for = 36,000 + 920,000 =	<u>956,000</u>
b.	Beginning inventory (36,000 x 100%)	36,000
	Started and completed [(945,000 - 36,000) x 100%]	909,000
	Ending inventory [(956,000 - 945,000) x 100%]	<u>11,000</u>
	Total EUP for direct material	<u>956,000</u>
c.	Beginning inventory (36,000 x 100%)	36,000
	Started and completed [909,000 x 100%]	909,000
	Ending inventory [11,000 x 30%]	<u>3,300</u>
	Total EUP for direct labour	<u>948,300</u>
d.	Beginning inventory (36,000 x 100%)	36,000
	Started and completed [909,000 x 100%]	909,000
	Ending inventory [11,000 x 5%]	<u>550</u>
	Total EUP for overhead	<u>945,550</u>

Exercise 16

a.

	DM	CONVERSION
Beginning inventory	42,000	42,000
S&C (150,000 - 42,000)	108,000	108,000
EI (100%; 60%)	30,000	18,000
Total EUP	180,000	168,000

b.

	DM	CONVERSION
Beginning inventory cost	$ 6,420	$ 7,056
Current cost	15,180	34,944
Total cost	$21,600	$ 42,000
Divided by EUP	÷ 180,000	÷ 168,000
Cost per EUP	$0.12	$0.25

c.

Transferred out = 150,000 x $0.37 =	$55,500
Ending inventory:	
Direct material (30,000 x $0.12)	$ 3,600
Conversion (30,000 x 60% x $0.25)	4,500
Cost of ending inventory	$ 8,100

Exercise 19

a.   Started & completed = 50,000 calendars
      (Transferred in - EWIP = 80,000 - 30,000 = 50,000 calendars)

	TI	DM	CONVERSION
BWIP (100%; 0%; 30%)	20,000	0	6,000
Added	----	20,000	14,000
Started and completed	50,000	50,000	50,000
EWIP (100%; 0%; 80%)	30,000	0	24,000
Total EUP	100,000	70,000	94,000

b.

	TI	DM	CONVERSION
BWIP cost	$ 25,000	$ 0	$ 1,114
Current costs	80,000	10,500	14,960
Total cost	$105,000	$10,500	$16,074
Divided by EUP	÷ 100,000	÷ 70,000	÷ 94,000
Cost per EUP	$1.05	$0.15	$0.171

c.   Cost transferred to Finished Goods Inventory = (70,000 x $1.371) = $95,970

d.

Cost of ending WIP inventory:	
Transferred in (30,000 x $1.05)	$31,500
Direct material (30,000 x 0% x $0.15)	0
Conversion (30,000 x 80% x $0.171)	4,104
Total cost of ending WIP inventory	$35,604

Exercise 21
Costs charged to Department B during October:

Transferred from Department A	$182,000
Materials	34,000
Conversion costs	222,950
Total	$438,950

Calculations

	Physical Units	Transferred In	Material	Conversion
Beginning inventory	3,000			
Started	20,000			
	23,000			
Finished	17,000	17,000	17,000	17,000
Normal spoilage	680	680	0	646
Abnormal spoilage	320	320	0	304
Ending inventory	5,000	5,000	0	3,500
	23,000	23,000	17,000	21,450

Costs	Total			
Beginning inventory	$ 38,000	$ 25,000	$ 0	$ 13,000
Current	438,950	182,000	34,000	222,950
Total	$476,950	$207,000	$34,000	$235,950
Unit costs	$22.00	$9.00	$2.00	$11

Costs Accounted For:

Finished (17,000 x $22.00)			$374,000
Normal spoilage (680 x $ 9.00)		$ 6,120	
(646 x $11.00)		7,106	13,226
			$387,226
Abnormal spoilage (320 x $ 9.00)		$ 2,880	
(304 x $11.00)		3,344	6,224
Ending inventory (5,000 x $ 9.00)		$ 45,000	
(3,500 x $11.00)		38,500	83,500
			$476,950

Exercise 22

a.	Work in Process Inventory-Dehydration	200,000	
	Raw Material Inventory		200,000
b.	Work in Process Inventory-Dehydration	160,000	
	Overhead-Dehydration	80,000	
	Wages Payable		240,000
c.	Overhead-Dehydration	140,000	
	Various accounts		140,000
d.	Work in Process Inventory-Pelletizing	660,000	
	Work in Process Inventory-Dehydration		660,000
e.	Work in Process Inventory-Pelletizing	124,000	
	Overhead-Pelletizing	38,000	
	Wages Payable		162,000
f.	Overhead-Pelletizing	226,000	
	Various accounts		226,000
g.	Finished Goods Inventory	980,000	
	Work in Process-Pelletizing		980,000
h.	Cost of Goods Sold	900,000	
	Finished Goods Inventory		900,000
	Cash	1,460,000	
	Sales		1,460,000

Exercise 24

a.	Beginning WIP inventory (40,000 x 40%)	16,000
	Started and completed [(200,000 - 40,000) x 100%]	160,000
	Ending WIP inventory (120,000 x 75%)	90,000
	Total EUP	266,000

b. Units transferred out = BWIP + Started - EWIP
    = 40,000 + 240,000 - 60,000 = 220,000

Beginning inventory (40,000 x 75%)	30,000
Started and completed [(220,000 - 40,000) x 100%]	180,000
Ending inventory (60,000 x 60%)	36,000
Total EUP	246,000

c. Ending inventory = BWIP + Started - Transferred
    = 15,000 + 135,000 - 130,000 = 20,000

Beginning WIP inventory (15,000 x 70%)	10,500
Started and completed [(130,000 - 15,000) x 100%]	115,000
Ending inventory (20,000 x 90%)	18,000
Total EUP	143,500

d. Units started = Transferred + EWIP - BWIP
    = 180,000 + 20,000 - 10,000 = 190,000

Beginning inventory (10,000 x 80%)	8,000
Started and completed [(180,000 - 10,000) x 100%]	170,000
Ending inventory (20,000 x 70%)	14,000
Total EUP	192,000

Exercise 26

Started & completed = Started - EWIP = 58,000 - 8,000 = 50,000

	DM	CONVERSION
Beginning WIP inventory (0%; 30%)	0	3,600
Started and completed	50,000	50,000
Ending WIP inventory (100%; 25%)	8,000	2,000
Total EUP	58,000	55,600

	DM	CONVERSION
Current cost	$172,840	$141,780
Divided by EUP	÷ 58,000	÷ 55,600
Cost per EUP	$2.98	$2.55

a. Transferred out:

Beginning WIP inventory cost	$ 61,780	
Cost to complete (3,600 x $2.55)	9,180	
Started & completed (50,000 x $5.53)	276,500	$347,460

b. Ending inventory:

Direct material (8,000 x $2.98)	$ 23,840	
Conversion (8,000 x 25% x $2.55)	5,100	$ 28,940

Exercise 28
a to d:

	Units	Material	Conversion
Beginning inventory	8.000		
Units started	180,000		
Units to account for	188,000		
Beginning inventory completed	8,000	6,400	5,600
Units started and completed	174,600	174,600	174,600
Total units transferred	182,600		
Ending inventory (70%; 80%)	4,000	2,800	3,200
Normal spoilage (180,000 x 0.4%)	720	0	0
Abnormal spoilage	680	680	680
Units accounted for (FIFO EUP)	188,000	184,480	184,080

e.   Cost of normal spoilage is automatically spread among all of the remaining units produced. This is done by using the method of neglect and omitting these spoiled units from the EUP calculations.

f.   Cost of abnormal spoilage is treated as a period cost.

PROBLEMS

Problem 1
Purchase of materials:

Raw Materials	900,000	
Accounts Payable		900,000

Issuance of materials into production:

Work in Process	500,000	
Manufacturing Overhead	200,000	
Raw Materials		700,000

Factory labour costs are incurred:

Work in Process	500,000	
Manufacturing Overhead	150,000	
Salaries and Wages Payable		650,000

Application of factory overhead:

Work in Process	550,000	
Manufacturing Overhead		550,000

Completion of Job #807:

Finished Goods	250,000	
Work in Process		250,000

Sale of Job #807:

Accounts Receivable	400,000	
Cost of Goods Sold	250,000	
Sales		400,000
Finished Goods		250,000

Problem 5
a. Calculation of cost per equivalent unit in Department B (weighted average)

	Transferred-In	Materials	Conversion	Total
Equivalent units:				
Transferred out	44,000	44,000	44,000	
Plus: Equivalent units in ending work in process				
Transferred in (16,000 x 1.0)	16,000			
Materials		0		
Conversion (16,000 x 3/8)			6,000	
	60,000	44,000	50,000	
Costs:				
In opening inventory of work in process	$9,500	$ 0	$ 11,200	
This period	45,600 [1]	13,200	63,000	
	$55,100	$ 13,200	$ 74,200	
Cost per equivalent unit	$ 0.92	$ 0.30	$ 1.48	$2.70

[1] [(44,000 + 16,000 - 12,000) x $0.95]

Cost of goods transferred out (weighted-average)
    44,000 x $2.70 = $118,800

b.   Cost of ending inventory of work in process

Transferred in (16,000 x $0.92)	$14,720
Materials	0
Conversion (6,000 x $1.48)	8,880
	$23,600

Problem 7

a	Beginning WIP inventory		12,000
	Units started this period		24,000
	Total units to account for		36,000

	Units to account for:		
	Units in ending inventory		17,000
	Units transferred to Finished Goods inventory		19,000
	Total units accounted for		36,000

		DM	CC
b.	Beginning inventory	12,000	12,000
	Started and completed	7,000	7,000
	Ending inventory	17,000	6,800
	EUP	36,000	25,800
c.	Beginning inventory	$ 9,500	$14,700
	Costs this period	35,600	73,080
	Total	$45,100	$87,780
d.	Total costs	$45,100	$87,780
	Divide by EUP	÷36,000	÷25,800
	Cost / EUP	$1.25	$3.40

e.	Cost of finished goods:	
	19,000 x ($1.25 + $3.40)	$88,350

	Cost of ending inventory:	
	DM	17,000 X $1.25 =$21,250
	Conversion:	6,800 X $3.40 = 23,120
	Total	$44,370

Problem 9
Cost of Production Report

(Weighted Average Method)

PRODUCTION DATA

EQUIVALENT UNITS OF PRODUCTION

	WHOLE UNITS	DM	CONVERSION
BWIP (100%; 40%)	1,500	1,500	600
Units started	56,000		
To account for	57,500		
BWIP completed	1,500	0	900
S&C	55,200	55,200	55,200
Units completed	56,700		
EWIP (100%; 80%)	800	800	640
Accounted for	57,500	57,500	57,340

COST DATA

	TOTAL	DM	CONVERSION
BWIP cost	$ 6,027	$ 2,440	$ 3,587
Current costs	180,648	112,560	68,088
Total cost to account for	$186,675	$115,000	$71,675
Divided by EUP		57,500	57,340
Cost per EUP	$3.25	$2.00	$1.25

COST ASSIGNMENT

Transferred out (56,700 x $3.25)			$184,275
Ending inventory:			
Direct material (800 x $2.00)		$1,600	
Conversion (640 X $1.25)		800	2,400
Total cost accounted for			$186,675

Problem 12

a.   Total units to account for = 20,000 + 100,000 = 120,000

b.   Number of units S&C = 100,000 - 25,000 = 75,000

c.   Total cost to account for = $785 + $915 + $15,190 + $8,400 = $25,290

d.

	DM	CONVERSION
Beginning WIP inventory (100%)	20,000	20,000
Started and completed	75,000	75,000
Ending WIP inventory (70%; 80%)	17,500	20,000
Total EUP	112,500	115,000

e.

	DM	CONVERSION
Beginning WIP inventory cost	$ 785	$ 915
Current cost	15,190	8,400
Total cost	$15,975	$ 9,315
Divided by EUP	÷ 112,500	÷ 115,000
Cost per EUP	$0.142	$0.081

f.

Transferred out = 95,000 x $0.223 =		$21,185
Ending WIP inventory:		
Direct material (17,500 x $.142)		$ 2,485
Conversion (20,000 x $0.081)		1,620
Cost of ending WIP inventory		$ 4,105

g.

	DM	CONVERSION
Beginning WIP inventory (80%; 50%)	16,000	10,000
Started and completed	75,000	75,000
Ending WIP inventory (70%; 80%)	17,500	20,000
Total EUP	108,500	105,000

h.

	DM	CONVERSION
Current cost	$15,190	$ 8,400
Divided by EUP	÷ 108,500	÷ 105,000
Cost per EUP	$0.14	$0.08

i.

Transferred out:		
Beginning WIP inventory cost	$ 1,700	
Cost to complete		
Material (16,000 x $0.14)	2,240	
Conversion (10,000 x $0.08)	800	
Started & completed (75,000 x $0.22)	16,500	$21,240
Ending WIP inventory:		
Direct material (17,500 x $0.14)	$ 2,450	
Conversion (20,000 x $0.08)	1,600	$ 4,050

Problem 15

a.
Cost of Production Report
(FIFO Method)

PRODUCTION DATA	WHOLE UNITS	EQUIVALENT UNITS OF PRODUCTION	
		DM	CONVERSION
BWIP (100%; 40%)	1,500	1,500	600
Units started	56,000		
To account for	57,500		
BWIP completed	1,500	0	900
S&C	55,200	55,200	55,200
Units completed	56,700		
EWIP (100%; 80%)	800	800	640
Accounted for	57,500	56,000	56,740

COST DATA	TOTAL	DM	CONVERSION
BWIP cost	$ 6,027		
Current costs	180,648	$112,560	$68,088
Total cost to account for	$186,675		
Divided by EUP		÷ 56,000	÷ 56,740
Cost per EUP	$3.21	$2.01	$1.20

COST ASSIGNMENT

Transferred out:		
BWIP costs	$ 6,027	
Cost to complete:		
Conversion (900 x $1.20)	1,080	
Total cost of BI transferred	$ 7,107	
S&C (55,200 x $3.21)	177,192	$184,299
Ending inventory:		
Direct material (800 x $2.01)	$ 1,608	
Conversion (640 x $1.20)	768	2,376
Total cost accounted for		$186,675

b. The beginning inventory cost per equivalent unit for conversion cost was ($3,587 ÷ 600) or $5.98. The current period conversion cost per EUP is $1.20. One possible explanation is that a significant reengineering effort took place in the department during this month, causing a drop in non-value-added activities and related costs. This situation is not exceptionally likely, however, because a reengineering effort of this magnitude would probably take several months to implement. A more probable explanation is that either costs were totally out of control in the prior month or that there has been a mistake in the cost information from either last period or this period.

Problem 17

a.

Cost of Production Report
(Weighted Average Method)

PRODUCTION DATA

EQUIVALENT UNITS OF PRODUCTION

	WHOLE UNITS	MAT. A	MAT. B	DL	OH
BWIP	*10,000	10,000	0	4,000	6,000
Units TI	80,000				
To account for	90,000				
BWIP completed	10,000	0	10,000	6,000	4,000
S&C	65,000	65,000	65,000	65,000	65,000
Units completed	75,000				
EWIP	**15,000	15,000	0	4,500	6,000
Accounted for	90,000	90,000	75,000	79,500	81,000

COST DATA

	TOTAL	MAT. A	MAT. B	DL	OH
BWIP cost	$ 4,625	$ 1,900	$ 0	$1,195	$ 1,530
Current costs	62,050	8,000	37,500	7,550	9,000
Total cost to account for	$66,675	$9,900	$37,500	$8,745	$10,530
Divided by EUP		÷ 90,000	÷ 75,000	÷ 79,500	÷ 81,000
Cost per EUP	$0.85	$0.11	$0.50	$0.11	$0.13

COST ASSIGNMENT

Transferred out (75,000 x $0.85)		$63,750
Ending WIP inventory:		
Material A (15,000 x $0.11)	$1,650	
Direct labour (4,500 x $0.11)	495	
Overhead (6,000 x $0.13)	780	2,925
Total cost accounted for		$66,675

*Fully complete as to material A; 0% as to material B; 40% as to labour; 60% as to overhead.

** Fully complete as to material A; 0% as to material B; 30% as to labour; 40% as to overhead.

Problem 19

a.   Manufacturing overhead rate = 1,050) 1,750 = 60% of direct labour costs

Applied overhead during November (29,000 X 0.6)	$ 17,400
Actual overhead during November	15,500
Over-applied overhead	$ 1,900

b.

(i) Weighted-Average Method

Equivalent Units	Transferred-In Costs	Direct Materials	Conversion Costs	Total
Completed	60,000	60,000	60,000	
Ending WIP	20,000	8,000	8,000	
Total costs	80,000	68,000	68,000	

Costs

	Transferred-In Costs	Direct Materials	Conversion Costs	Total
Beginning WIP	$ 10,875	$ 1,750	$ 2,800	
Added	69,125	15,750	46,400	
	$ 80,000	$ 17,500	$ 49,200	
Cost/Equivalent Unit	$1.00	$0.26	$0.72	$1.98

Transferred out: 60,000 x $1.98 = $118,800

(ii) FIFO Method

Equivalent Units	Transferred-In Costs	Direct Materials	Conversion Costs	Total
Beginning WIP	$ 0	$ 0	$ 4,000	
Started and completed	50,000	50,000	50,000	
Ending WIP	20,000	8,000	8,000	
	70,000	58,000	62,000	
Costs Added	$ 69,125	$15,750	$ 46,400	
Cost/Equivalent Unit	$ 0.99	$0.27	$0.75	$2.01

Transferred out:

Beginning WIP ($10,875 + $1,750 + $2,800)	$ 15,425
Costs to complete beginning WIP (4,000 x $0.75)	3,000
Started and completed 50,000 x $2.01	100,500
	$ 118,925

c.   The weighted-average costs of the ending WIP inventory for November:

Transferred-in (20,000 x $1.00)	$ 20,000
Direct materials (8,000 x $0.26)	2,080
Conversion costs (8,000 x $0.72)	5,760
	$ 27,840

d.   The FIFO cost/unit is higher than the weighted-average cost/unit. This would indicate that prices are increasing. Consequently, since weighted-average includes costs of last month's WIP, which is lower than the current month's costs, FIFO will result in a higher cost of ending WIP inventory.

CHAPTER 5
INTRODUCTION TO A STANDARD COST SYSTEM

QUESTIONS

1. A standard costing system is a planning tool because it ties in with the organization's financial budgets. The standard costs represent an expectation about what actual costs should be. The standard costing system's contribution to organizational control involves the comparison of the actual costs incurred for a period to the standard costs. Managers will investigate substantial deviations between actual and standard costs and take actions to bring them into alignment.

3. Standards are necessary for each cost component of a product or service so that the most detailed variance analysis can be conducted. Standards for the monetary amount and quantity of each cost component allow separate comparisons to actual figures and provide managers with the best means of determining what went "wrong" or "right" during the period. Such determinations are critical to correcting problems or instituting new methodologies for improvement.

4. A predetermined overhead rate is considered a standard because that rate has been developed as the accepted basis on which to assign estimated or budgeted overhead using an appropriate activity driver. Thus, it represents the "norm" per unit of activity measure.

6. Variance analysis is the process of categorizing the nature of favourable and unfavourable differences between standard and actual costs and seeking the reasons for those differences. Managers use the information as a means to focus their control efforts. By concentrating their attention on areas in which there are large differences between standard and actual costs, managers can take actions to move actual costs into alignment with the standards.

8. If the material price variance is computed on the basis of quantity of material purchased rather than used, a total material variance cannot be calculated because the material quantity variance will be calculated on a different base-- making a combination of the variances meaningless.

10. A large favourable labour rate variance may have occurred because you have employed less-skilled workers. If this were the case, you would expect the labour efficiency variance to be significantly unfavourable because the workers would probably produce many defective units or work more slowly than their more highly paid counterparts.

12.   This statement is false. Although consideration should be givens to the ease of obtaining a measurement in the production area, overhead standards should be set first on the basis of the most reasonable cost driver. If this measure is the most logical but is unavailable, accounting and data processing personnel should work together to determine a method of data collection, or select a reasonable alternative.

14.   No. Fixed overhead is generally incurred in lump-sum amounts and is only allocated to products on a per-unit basis for product costing purposes. Managers may be able to influence or control the quantity of production and, in that manner, the fixed cost per unit, but they cannot control fixed overhead on a per-unit basis.

16.   a.   The material price variance can be calculated at point of purchase or point of use and is the responsibility of the purchasing agent. Firms using traditional inventory management techniques will probably compute the variance based on quantity purchased. Firms that have adopted just-in-time (JIT) techniques will prefer to compute the variance based on the quantity used so that there will be no incentive to purchase materials for which there is no current production need.

       b.   The material quantity variance should be calculated at point of issuance of materials. This variance is typically the responsibility of the production supervisor.

  c. & d.   The labour rate and labour efficiency variances should be computed as payroll is recorded or assigned to Work in Process Inventory. These variances are also normally the responsibility of the production supervisor.

       e.   The variable overhead spending variance is usually calculated at the end of the month or the end of an accounting period. The variable overhead spending variance is primarily the responsibility of the production support personnel using the resources—especially if resources have been wasted.

       f.   The volume variance is usually calculated at the end of the month or the end of an accounting period. The volume variance is the responsibility of the production supervisor who controls scheduling. Some amount of volume variance may be planned for, depending on demand.

             Although the above assignments of responsibility are the usual ones, there may be exceptions. Some variances are interrelated, such as an unfavourable material quantity variance caused by inferior material quality and an unfavourable labour efficiency variance caused by reworking items made from the low-quality material. Labour rates may not be under the control of the production supervisor, but possibly the result of a new labour contract. Managers must look for underlying relationships when investigating both favourable and unfavourable variances.

18.   ERP systems increase the accuracy and prevalence of standards. These consequences occur because ERP systems use common charts of accounts and standard practices and data definitions to provide comparable data among the various parts of an organization, integrate activities and information from all parts of an organization, and keep accurate record of costs in numerous cost pools and allocate those costs with more accuracy.

20.   (Appendix) If the variances are insignificant, they are closed to Cost of Goods Sold or Cost of Services Rendered. This disposition is acceptable because the cost-benefit criterion would not support the time and effort that allocation to related accounts would take.

EXERCISES
Exercise 1
a.	3	f.	7
b.	8	g.	2
c.	6	h.	10
d.	1	i.	5
e.	9	j.	4

Exercise 3
a.   1.   Material price variance based on quantity purchased =
136,500 litres x ($14.50 − $13.90) = $81,900 U

2.   Material price variance based on quantity used =
130,500 litres x ($14.50 − $13.90) = $78,300 U

b.   Material quantity variance = $13.90 x (130,500 − 132,900) = $33,360 F

c.   A labour rate variance cannot be computed on two different bases because labour, unlike material, cannot be purchased in advance of use and stored.

Exercise 9
a.

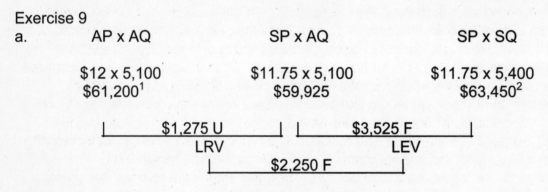

AP x AQ	SP x AQ	SP x SQ
$12 x 5,100	$11.75 x 5,100	$11.75 x 5,400
$61,200[1]	$59,925	$63,450[2]

$1,275 U	$3,525 F
LRV	LEV

$2,250 F

Total Labour Variance

[1] total labour cost
[2] standard labour cost

b.   To: Mr. Madden

After analyzing the labour variances, it appears that because the workers are being paid $0.25 per hour more than standard they are working more rapidly than expected. As you can see, you actually saved over $2,000 in this period on labour costs. It is my suggestion that this practice be continued. As well, a new, faster standard should be set for quilt-making time.

Exercise 12

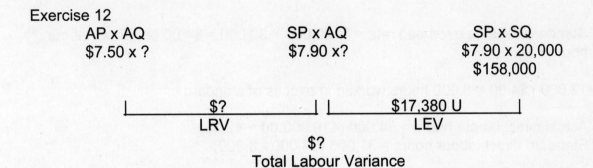

AP x AQ	SP x AQ	SP x SQ
$7.50 x ?	$7.90 x?	$7.90 x 20,000
		$158,000

$?	$17,380 U
LRV	LEV

$?
Total Labour Variance

a.   The middle column total is $158,000 + $17,380 or $175,380. Dividing $175,380 by the $7.90 standard rate per hour gives actual hours worked of <u>22,200</u>.

b.   The total payroll is equal to the 22,200 actual hours worked multiplied by the $7.50 actual rate per hour or <u>$166,500</u>.

c.   The labour rate variance equals the $166,500 total payroll minus the $175,380 total of the middle column or $8,880 F. This amount can also be calculated as 22,200 x ($7.50 - $7.90).

d.   To: Mr. Silva
Re: Employee motivation
Prior to any changes to your standards, an open discussion should take place with your direct labour employees to ascertain their concerns and viewpoints of the situation. Productivity may be low because the machines are in need of maintenance or can no longer handle the volume of product output. Should those issues not be valid, it appears that your employees are working at a lower efficiency level than you would like because they are being paid less than your designated standard wage rate. We would suggest raising direct labour pay to the $7.90 per hour standard and monitor whether this has the effect of increasing productivity. If not, additional training should be provided. Alternatively, if employees are left at the $7.50 per hour rate, you may want to consider using a lower standard quantity of time per production unit.

Exercise 15

a. $12,000 ÷ 0.10 = 120,000 kg.

b. $7,500 ÷ 3.00 = 2,500 kg

c. $360,000 ÷ 30,000 hours = $12.00 per hour

d.   Standard variable overhead rate = $120,000 ÷ 30,000 = $4.00 per direct labour hour

12,000) $4.00 = 3,000 hours worked in excess of standard

Actual direct labour hours = 34,000 (419,900.00 ÷ 12.35)
Standard direct labour hours = 31,000 (34,000 - 3,000) .

(Exercise 15 is adapted by the authors from *Management Accounting Examinations*, published by the Certified General Accountants' Association of Canada © CGA-Canada, 1994, used by permission.)

Exercise 16
a.   Standard quantity allowed = (1,800 units x 15 minutes) ÷ 60 minutes per hour = 450 MHs
        Total applied VOH = $14 x 450 MHs = $6,300

b.
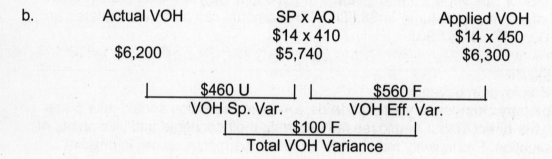

Actual VOH	SP x AQ	Applied VOH
	$14 x 410	$14 x 450
$6,200	$5,740	$6,300

| $460 U | $560 F |
| VOH Sp. Var. | VOH Eff. Var. |
| $100 F |
| Total VOH Variance |

c.   It is possible that the standard quantity of machine time is obsolete and needs to be changed to reflect new skills by workers, new machine technology, or new factory layout.

Exercise 18
a.   Total standard DLHs = (100 X 10) + (400 X 3) + (60 X 12) = 2,920 DLHs
        Total applied VOH = $4 X 2,920 = $11,680

b.
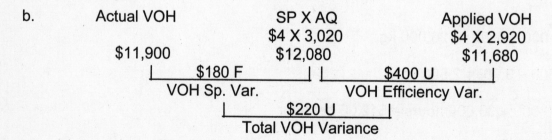

Actual VOH	SP X AQ	Applied VOH
	$4 X 3,020	$4 X 2,920
$11,900	$12,080	$11,680

| $180 F | $400 U |
| VOH Sp. Var. | VOH Efficiency Var. |
| $220 U |
| Total VOH Variance |

c.   Direct labour hours are not normally a reasonable application base in an automated plant. In such an environment, workers normally are cross-trained and tend to operate machines that perform the majority of the actual manufacturing work on the product. Machine hours, setup time, or other more technology-based items would be better application bases.

Exercise 21

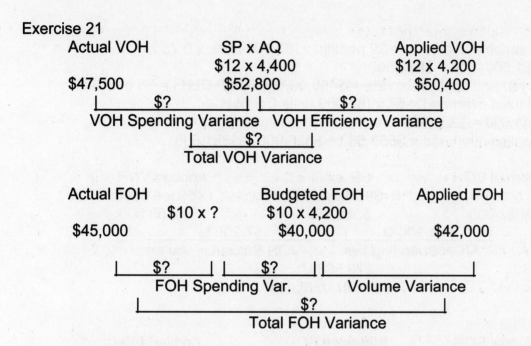

a.   Total actual overhead cost = Actual VOH + Actual FOH = $47,500 + $45,000 = <u>$92,500</u>

b.   Total applied overhead = Applied VOH + Applied FOH = ($12 x 4,200) + ($10 x $4,200) = $50,400 + $42,000 = <u>$92,400</u>

c.   VOH spending variance = $47,500 - $52,800 = <u>$5,300 F</u>
     VOH efficiency variance = $52,800 - $50,400 = <u>$2,400 U</u>
     Total VOH variance = <u>$2,900 F</u>

d.   FOH spending variance = $45,000 - $40,000 = <u>$5,000 U</u>
     Volume variance = $40,000 - $42,000 = <u>$2,000 F</u>
     Total FOH variance = <u>$3,000 U</u>

Exercise 24

a.   Applied variable overhead = $9 per kilo x (82,000 units x 0.75 kilos)
        = $9 x 61,500 kilos = $553,500
        Fixed overhead application rate = $480,000 ÷ 60,000 DLHs = $8 per DLH;
        Applied fixed overhead = $8 x (82,000 units 0.5 DLH)
        = $8 x 41,000 = $328,000
        Total applied overhead = $553,500 + $328,000 = $881,500

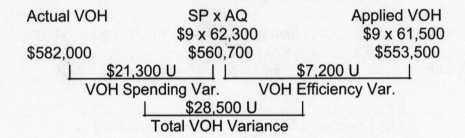

Actual VOH	SP x AQ $9 x 62,300	Applied VOH $9 x 61,500
$582,000	$560,700	$553,500

| $21,300 U | $7,200 U |
          VOH Spending Var.   VOH Efficiency Var.
                        | $28,500 U |
                                Total VOH Variance

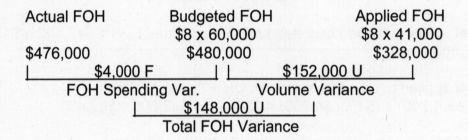

Actual FOH	Budgeted FOH $8 x 60,000	Applied FOH $8 x 41,000
$476,000	$480,000	$328,000

| $4,000 F | $152,000 U |
          FOH Spending Var.   Volume Variance
                        | $148,000 U |
                                Total FOH Variance

b.   To: Ms Poë:

The products made during this year appear to have been heavier than in the past
(more kilograms used than standard), which could have resulted in the need for
additional worker time and wages to move the units, possibly causing the
unfavourable VOH spending variance. Also, actual production was significantly
less than had been budgeted, but fixed overhead costs are committed in
advance of production. Thus, the company was unable to get out of the majority
of its obligations and realized a large, unfavourable FOH volume variance. Actual
FOH spending was slightly below budget, generating a $4,000 favourable FOH
spending variance.

Exercise 26

a.   **Direct materials:**
        Price variance: 5,000 x (3.10 - 3.00) = $500 U
        Quantity variance: 3.00 x (4,800 - 4,600) = $600 F

        Direct labour:
        Rate variance: 1,950 x (16.50 - 16.00) = $975 U
        Efficiency variance: 16.00 x (1,800 - 1,950) = $2,400 U

Variable overhead:
Spending variance: 19,000 - (1,950 x 10.00) = $500 F
Efficiency variance: (1,800 x 10.00) - 19,500 = $1,500 U

Fixed overhead:
Spending variance: 10,000 - 9,000 = $1,000 U
Volume variance: 9,000 - (1,800 x $4.00) = $1,800 U

b.   The $1,800 unfavourable production volume arose because 1,200 units were produced during August instead of 1,500. Moose Jaw produced 300 units less than expected. With a fixed overhead rate of $6.00/unit, $1,800 of fixed overhead was not absorbed by the August production.

Exercise 29
a.   Materials price variance:
        6,000 ($20.00 - $19.95) = $300 F

Materials quantity variance:
        $20.00 (5,100 - 5,000) = $2,000 U

Labour rate variance:
        1,960 ($12.40 - $12.00) = $784 U

Labour efficiency variance:
        $12.00 (2,000 - 1,960) = $480 F

Variable overhead spending variance:
        $16,001 - (1,960 x $8.00) = $321 U

Variable overhead efficiency variance:
        $8.00 (2,000 - 1,960) = $320 F

Fixed overhead spending variance:
        $58,000 - (2,400 x $25.00) = $2,000 F

Volume variance:
        $25.00 (2,400 - 2,000) = $10,000 U

b.   Materials price variance:

	Litres	Variance
Raw Materials Inventory	900 (6,000 - 5,100)	45
Work in process inventory	0	0
Finished goods	1,020 (5,100 X 20%)	51
Cost of goods sold	4,080 (5,100 X 80%)	204
Total	6,000	300 F

All other variances:

	Units	**Variances**
Finished goods	200	$2,061
Cost of goods sold	800	8,244
Total	1,000	$10,305 U

Cost of goods sold:
(800 x $190) - 204 + 8,244 = $160,040

Alternative Solution Method:
Actual costs:

Materials (5,100 x 19.95)	$101,745
Direct labour	24,304
Variable overhead	16,001
Fixed overhead	58,000
Cost of goods manufactured	$200,050

Cost of good sold:
80% of 200,050 = $160,040

PROBLEMS

Problem 1

	Case 1	Case 2	Case 3	Case 4
Units produced	500	9,000	(g)	1,760
Std. litres per unit	(a)	(d)	12.5	10.6
Std. price per litre	$0.90	(e)	$1.30	(j)
Std. quantity allowed	10,000	36,000	(h)	(k)
Act. quantity purchased	(b)	34,900	4,900	20,000
Act. quantity used	9,800	36,450	4,895	18,450
Act. price per litre	$0.92	$5.04	(l)	$2.55
MPV	$214 U	$1,396 U	$490 F	(l)
MQV	(c)	(f)	$26 U	$515 F

a.   Standard litres per unit = 10,000 ÷ 500 = <u>20 litres</u>

b. $214 U = Actual quantity purchased x ($0.92 - $0.90);
      Actual quantity purchased = $214 U ÷ $0.02 = <u>10,700 litres</u>

c.   Material quantity variance = (10,000 - 9,800) x $0.90 = <u>$180 F</u>

d.   Standard litres per unit = Standard quantity allowed ÷ Units produced
      = 36,000 ÷ 9,000 = <u>4 litres</u>

e.   Total actual cost of material purchased = 34,900 x $5.04 = $175,896;
      $175,896 - $1,396 U material price variance = $174,500 standard price of
      material purchased; $174,500 ÷ 34,900 litres purchased = <u>$5 standard price per
      litre</u>

f.   Material quantity variance = $5 x (36,450 - 36,000) = <u>$2,250 U</u>

h.   (Must do before part g)

      Standard quantity allowed: Material quantity variance =
      Standard price x (actual quantity used - standard quantity allowed);
      $26 U = $1.30 (4,895 - ?) = <u>4,875 litres</u>

g.   Units produced = 4,875 ÷ 12.5 = <u>390 units</u>

i.   Actual price per litre: Material price variance = Actual quantity purchased x
      (actual price - standard price); $490 F = 4,900($? - $1.30) = <u>$1.20 per litre</u>

k.   (Must do before part j)
      Standard quantity allowed = 1,760 x 10.6 = <u>18,656 litres</u>

j.   Standard price per litre: Material quantity variance =
        Standard price x (actual quantity used - standard quantity allowed);
        $515 F = $? (18,450 - 18,656) = <u>$2.50 per litre</u>

l.   Material price variance = 20,000 x ($2.55 - $2.50) = <u>$1,000 U</u>

Problem 4
a.   Material price variance = 115,000 X ($1.70 - $2.10) = <u>$46,000 F</u>

        Standard quantity allowed = 39,600 boxes x 2 square metres
        = 79,200 square metres

        Material quantity variance = $2.10 (88,500 - 79,200) = <u>$19,530 U</u>

b.   Standard quantity of time allowed = (39,600 boxes x 10 minutes) ÷ 60
        = 6,600 DLHs

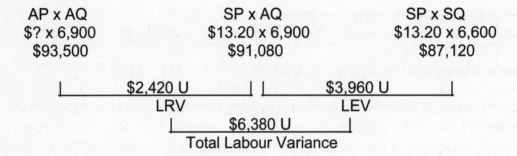

AP x AQ	SP x AQ	SP x SQ
$? x 6,900	$13.20 x 6,900	$13.20 x 6,600
$93,500	$91,080	$87,120

| $2,420 U | | $3,960 U |
| LRV | | LEV |
| $6,380 U |
| Total Labour Variance |

c.   To: Christopher Cowan, Controller

        After reviewing the material and labour variances for May, I have decided that the
        majority of the items (with the exception of the labour rate variance) may be
        related. The significant favourable material price variance was caused by the fact
        that I unknowingly obtained a lower-grade material than called for in the product
        specifications. This created a need for excessive use and substantial rework for
        the employees. I had been assured by the supplier that the material was as called
        for in the product specs; we will no longer be using this company as a supplier of
        choice.

Problem 9

a.   Material price variance:

Actual quantity of material purchased = $7,152) $14.90 = 480 metres
Standard quantity of material allowed = 1.5 metres x 300 bags = 450 metres

Standard price x (Actual quantity - Standard quantity)
= Material quantity variance; Standard price ($480 - $450) = $450 U;
Standard price = $15 per metre

MPV = 480 x ($14.90 - $15.00) = <u>$48 F</u>
Standard time allowed = 300 bags x 3 hours = 900 DLHs
Labour efficiency variance = $9 x (880 - 900) = <u>$180 F</u>

b.   Standard cost of material $22.50   (1.5 metres x $15 per metre)
Standard cost of labour $27.00 (3 hours x $9 per hour)

Total standard prime cost   <u>$49.50</u>

c.   To: Mr. Wong, President
Re: Variance analysis for June 2008

During the month, the cost for direct material ($14.90) was slightly less than
normal ($15). This discrepancy could have been related to a slightly lower grade
of material, causing the unfavourable material quantity variance.* In the area of
labour, wage rates were higher than standard, but efficiency was up. Perhaps
more skilled workers were able to work more productively than planned.

* (more material was needed to produce output)

Problem 12

a.   i. $715,000 ÷ $6.50 = 110,000
      ii.   110,000 ÷ 0.2 = 550,000 shades
      iii. $17,000 F = Budgeted Fixed Overhead – ($110,000 x $6.50)
              Budgeted Fixed Overhead = $698,000
      iv. $698,000 ÷ $6.50 = $107,385
      v. $709,000 – $698,000 = $11,000
      vi. $709,000 – (110,000 x $6.50) = $6,000 F

b.   i.   110,000 MH X $8.50 = $935,000
      ii.   Actual VOH – Applied VOH = $937,400 - $935,000 = $2,400 U
      iii.   Actual VOH – Budgeted VOH = VOH spending variance;
              $937,400 – Budgeted VOH = $10,900 U; Budgeted VOH = $926,500
              Budgeted VOH = Actual MHs x $8.50; $926,500 = Actual MHs x $8.50;
              Actual MHs = 109,000 MHs

iv. VOH efficiency variance = Budgeted VOH – Applied VOH = $926,500 - $935,000 = $8,500 F

c.   An unfavourable variable overhead spending variance can be caused by either using too much of the inputs that comprise variable overhead or by paying too much for those items. For controlling the usage of items, the president should talk to the production manager regarding the prices paid for the items used and the president would want to talk to the purchasing department manager.

Problem 15

a.   Standard hours allowed = 4,200 x 3 = <u>12,600 MHs</u>

b.   VOH application rate = $9,600 ÷ (4,000 X 3) = $0.80 per MH

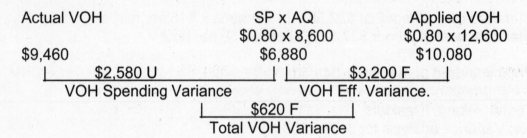

Actual VOH	SP x AQ	Applied VOH
	$0.80 x 8,600	$0.80 x 12,600
$9,460	$6,880	$10,080

|_____$2,580 U_____| |_____$3,200 F_____|
   VOH Spending Variance   VOH Eff. Variance.
                  |_____$620 F_____|
                        Total VOH Variance

FOH application rate = $24,000 ÷ (4,000 X 3) = $2 per MH

Actual FOH	Budgeted FOH	Applied FOH
		$2 X12,600
$24,900	$24,000	$25,200

|_____$900 U_____| |_____$1,200 F_____|
      FOH Sp. Variance   Volume Variance.
                  |_____$300 F_____|
                        Total FOH Variance

c.   The standards that would be affected include the following:

- Material quantity standard--would likely be tightened to reflect less waste, scrap, and rejects; may need to be modified to reflect new required materials.
- Labour rate standard--might be increased to reflect a higher required skill to operate the more complex technology
- Labour quantity standard -would likely be increased to reflect higher levels of efficiency associated with the new technology
- Variable overhead rate--would be adjusted to reflect the operating costs of the new machinery and, possibly, depreciation on the new machinery if calculated on a machine hour or usage basis; might also be adjusted to reflect lower quality appraisal costs.

- Budgeted fixed overhead--would be increased to reflect all fixed costs (including depreciation, if calculated on a straight-line basis) associated with the new technology.

In addition to general managers, the vendor of the new technology would be consulted as to the operating costs of the machinery and the learning curve for workers operating the machinery; labour experts would be consulted to develop new labour standards; engineering specialists would be consulted to develop a new material quantity standard; and accountants would be involved to translate the information from functional experts into dollars.

Problem 17

a.   Standard cost = 8,500 x ($0.08 + $0.38 + $1.20 + $0.80 + $1.10)
= 8,500 x $3.56 = $30,260.

$31,600 actual cost - $30,260 standard cost = $1,340 U

Total actual cost of materials purchased = $864 + $1,500 + $1,740 = $4,104
Total standard cost of actual materials purchased
= [($0.40 x 1,800) + ($0.38 x 9,000)] = $720 + $3,420 = $4,140

$$\text{AP x AQ} \qquad \text{SP x AQ}$$
$$\$4,104 \qquad\qquad \$4,140$$
$$|\underline{\qquad \text{MPV} \qquad}|$$
$$\$36 \text{ F}$$

Total standard cost of actual materials used = $760 + $2,280 + $1,330 = $4,370

b.   Total standard cost of standard quantity of materials =
($0.40 x 8,500 x 0.2) + ($0.38 x 8,500 x 1.0) = $680 + $3,230 = $3,910

$$\text{SP x AQ} \qquad\qquad\qquad \text{SP x SQ}$$
$$\$4,370 \qquad\qquad\qquad\qquad \$3,910$$
$$|\underline{\qquad\qquad \text{MQV} \qquad\qquad}|$$
$$\$460 \text{ U}$$

Total actual cost of labour = $9,200 + $2,400 = $11,600
Standard DL hours allowed = 8,500 x 0.3 = 2,550

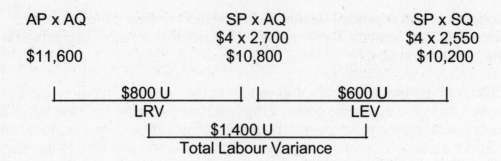

AP x AQ	SP x AQ	SP x SQ
	$4 x 2,700	$4 x 2,550
$11,600	$10,800	$10,200

$800 U	$600 U
LRV	LEV

$1,400 U
Total Labour Variance

c.   Standard machine hours allowed = 8,500 x0.5 = 4,250

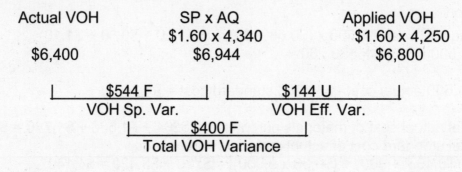

Actual VOH	SP x AQ	Applied VOH
	$1.60 x 4,340	$1.60 x 4,250
$6,400	$6,944	$6,800

$544 F	$144 U
VOH Sp. Var.	VOH Eff. Var.

$400 F
Total VOH Variance

Monthly budgeted FOH = [(48,000 MHs x $2.20)) 12] = $8,800

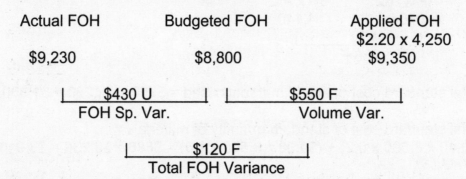

Actual FOH	Budgeted FOH	Applied FOH
		$2.20 x 4,250
$9,230	$8,800	$9,350

$430 U	$550 F
FOH Sp. Var.	Volume Var.

$120 F
Total FOH Variance

d.   The unfavourable quantity variance is likely related to the purchase of inferior quality plastic which caused a number of sprinklers to be rejected upon inspection.

e.   To: President, David Faber Mfg. Company
       Re: February production variances

       This month's total variance was unfavourable. This situation was most probably caused in large part by the purchase of 6,000 kilos of low grade plastic. This purchase was necessitated by an industry shortage of plastics. The company might have protected itself from this purchase by foreseeing this shortage and purchasing appropriate quantities in advance of the shortage. Such a purchase, however would have required the company to incur storage costs for the plastic.

This cost would be balanced against the costs of producing rejected product and creating potential damage to the company's reputation. Because plastic is an oil-based product and oil quantities are often subject to the "whims" of foreign oil companies, it is suggested that the company investigate options to prevent this situation from recurring in the future.

(CMA adapted)

Problem 20

a   Standard cost card for one water test:

Material test kits ($3.80 x 2)		$ 7.60
Direct labour [$22.80 x (10 ÷ 60)]		3.80
Overhead:		
Variable	$ 4.80	
Fixed ($69,000 ÷ 10,000)	6.90	11.70
Total standard cost per test		$23.10

b.   Materials price and quantity variances:

Actual material costs incurred	$70,300
Standard price x actual quantity purchased	
$3.80 x 19,000	72,200
Materials price variance (favourable)	$ 1,900

Standard price x actual quantity used	$70,300
Standard price x standard quantity allowed	
[$3.80 x (9,000 x 2)]	68,400
Materials quantity variance (unfavourable)	$ 1,900

Direct labour rate and efficiency variances:

Direct payroll	$37,646.00
Standard rate x actual hours ($22.80 x 1,623)	37,004.40
Labour rate variance (unfavourable)	$ 641.60

Standard rate x actual hours	$37,004.40
Standard rate x standard hours allowed	
[$22.80 x (9,000 x 10 ÷ 60)]	34,200.00
Labour efficiency variance (unfavourable)	$ 2,804.40

c.   Laboratory variable overhead variances:

Actual variable overhead costs	$45,200.00
Budgeted variable overhead for 1,623 hours	
[($4.80 x 6) x 1,623]	46,742.40
Variable overhead spending variance (favourable)	$ 1,542.40

Budgeted variable overhead for 1,623 hours $ 46,742.40
Budgeted variable overhead for 9,000 tests
($4.80 x 9,000)   43,200.00
Variable overhead efficiency variance (unfavourable) $ 3,542.40

(CMA adapted)

Problem 24

a.   Standard quantity of blades = 5,400 X 2 = 10,800
     Standard quantity of kits = 5,400 X 1 = 5,400
     Standard grinding labour time = 5,400 X ½ = 2,700 DLHs
     Standard finishing labour time = 5,400 X 2/3 = 3,600 DLHs
     Standard machine time = ½ hour per kit = 2,700 MHs

     Material price variance
     = [($12.75 X 11,300) + ($5.60 X 5,900)] - [($13 X 11,300) + ($6 X 5,900)]
     = ($144,075 + $33,040) - ($146,900 + $35,400)
     = $177,115 - $182,300
     = $5,185 F

     Material quantity variance
     = [($13 X 10,900) + ($6 X 5,650)] - [($13 X 10,800) + ($6 X 5,400)]
     = ($141,700 + $33,900) - ($140,400 + $32,400)
     = $175,600 - $172,800
     = $2,800 U

     Labour rate variance
     = ($42,000 + $45,325) - [($14 X 2,800) + ($12 X 3,700)]
     = $87,325 - ($39,200 + $44,400)
     = $87,325 - $83,600
     = $3,725 U

     Labour efficiency variance
     = $83,600 - [($14 X 2,700) + ($12 X 3,600)]
     = $83,600 - ($37,800 + $43,200)
     = $83,600 - $81,000
     = $2,600 U

Actual VOH	SP x AQ	Applied VOH
	$8 x 2,900	$8 x 2,700

$22,910	$23,200	$21,600

└────── $290 F ──────┘	└────── $1,600 U ──────┘
VOH Sp. Variance	VOH Eff. Variance.

Budgeted FOH = (5,000 kits X ½ hour X $12) = $30,000

Actual FOH	Budgeted FOH	Applied FOH
		$12 x 2,700
$33,000	$30,000	$32,400

└────── $3,000 U ──────┘	└────── $2,400 F ──────┘
FOH Sp. Variance	Volume Variance

i.	Raw Material Inventory	182,300	
	Accounts Payable		177,115
	Material Price Variance		5,185
ii.	Work in Process Inventory	172,800	
	Material Quantity Variance	2,800	
	Raw Material Inventory		175,600
iii.	Work in Process Inventory	81,000	
	Labour Rate Variance	3,725	
	Labour Efficiency Variance	2,600	
	Wages Payable		87,325
iv.	Manufacturing Overhead	55,910	
	Various accounts		55,910
v.	Work in Process Inventory	54,000	
	Variable Overhead		21,600
	Fixed Overhead		32,400
vi.	VOH Efficiency Variance	1,600	
	FOH Spending Variance	3,000	
	VOH Spending Variance		290
	Volume Variance		2,400
	Manufacturing Overhead		1,910
vii.	Finished Goods Inventory	307,800	
	Work in Process Inventory		307,800

viii.	Accounts Receivable	425,000	
	Sales		425,000
	Cost of Goods Sold[1]	228,000	
	Finished Goods Inventory		228,000

[1](307,800) 5,400 X 4,000)

b.	Material Price Variance	5,185	
	VOH Spending Variance	290	
	Volume Variance	2,400	
	Cost of Goods Sold	5,850	
	Material Quantity Variance		2,800
	Labour Rate Variance		3,725
	Labour Efficiency Variance		2,600
	VOH Efficiency Variance		1,600
	FOH Spending Variance		3,000

c. Except for the material price variance, all variances would be prorated among cost of goods sold and finished goods inventory (work in process inventory is $0) based on their respective closing balances. The material price variance would be allocated to the accounts just mentioned as well as raw material inventory.

CHAPTER 6
ACTIVITY-BASED MANAGEMENT AND COSTING

Questions

1. Product cost information is necessary to allow managers to accomplish two functions: (1) financial reporting of inventories and cost of goods sold; and (2) effective and efficient conduct of the managerial functions of planning, controlling, evaluating, and decision making (such as pricing).

3. Value-added activities increase the worth of a product or service in the eyes of the consumer. Non-value-added activities increase the time spent on a product or service but do not increase its value in the eyes of the consumer. Performing tasks required for production (adding materials, blending, molding, assembling, and so forth) are value-added activities; moving partially completed units of inventory, storing parts, inspecting for quality, and allowing parts to sit and wait to be worked on are examples of non-value-added activities.

5. Cycle efficiency measures operational efficiency. In a manufacturing environment, cycle efficiency is calculated as value-added processing time divided by total cycle time. The numerator refers to the actual time it takes to physically manufacture a unit. Total cycle time is value-added time plus all time spent on non-value-added activities, such as inspection time, transfer time, and idle time. In an optimized manufacturing environment, the non-value-added activities would be eliminated so the value of the MCE would be 100 percent.

    In a service environment, cycle efficiency is calculated as value-added service time divided by total cycle time. The numerator refers to the actual time it takes to actually provide service to the customer (e.g. paint a house or shingle a roof). Total cycle time is the time from the placement of a service order to service completion.

7. Yes, cost drivers exist in conventional accounting systems although they are generally called *allocation bases*. In conventional systems, a single cost driver such as direct labour hours or machine hours is commonly used rather than multiple cost drivers. Also in conventional systems, volume-based cost drivers are more the norm than non-volume-based cost drivers, such as square footage. Finally, conventional accounting stresses finding an allocation base that demonstrates strong statistical correlation to the cost, but ABC emphasizes searching for multiple cost drivers that bear cause-and-effect relationships to the cost.

9.   The four levels of cost drivers are unit, batch, product/process, and organizational/facility. The traditional costing system assumes that costs are all incurred at the unit level. Activity-based costing requires costs to be aggregated at different levels because the activities that cause costs to be generated occur at different levels. Only if costs are accumulated on the same level as the activity that generates them can an allocation base be selected that represents a cause–effect relationship between the cost and the cost pool.

11.   By using a single cost pool and a single cost driver to allocate overhead, the more traditional methods of overhead assignment ignore the influence on cost of the different activities that occur to make a product. In this manner, low-volume specialty products, which cause a disproportionate amount of overhead, are assigned only an average charge for overhead, thereby shifting costs to the standard product lines. ABC does a better job of tracing costs to the products that caused such costs by using multiple cost pools and multiple cost drivers.

15   In ABC, control is exerted on the cause of a cost which is the activity and its cost driver, whereas in conventional costing, control is focused on the cost itself. Control of the source of a cost is the more effective way to control the cost. This is analogous to treating the cause, rather than the symptoms, of an illness.

16.   ABC is not widely used for cost assignment in external reporting because (a) the new costs would not significantly affect income or assets; (b) the system is not used firm-wide and, thus, makes internal comparisons difficult; and (c) the new costs may not be fully consistent with generally accepted accounting principles or Canada Revenue Agency's regulations.

19.   Yes. ABC systems are integrated parts of ERP systems. In being integrated, the output of ABC systems will be consistent with the remainder of the ERP outputs, including financial statements.

EXERCISES

Exercise 1
a.   10   f.   7
b.   9   g.   1
c.   8   h.   6
d.   2   i.   4
e.   3   j.   5

Exercise 3
a.   Value-added activities add value to the clients.
- Take depositions
- Do legal research
- Making calls concerning caseA
- Litigate case
- Write correspondence, if necessary to litigation strategy or results in desired action for the client
- Contemplate litigation strategies, if enhances ideas and results in better litigation
- Write wills

b.   Non-value-added activities are non-essential to client work.
- Travel to/from court
- Eat lunch with clients, unless discussion relates to case and results in something of value
- Eat dinner at office while watching Jeopardy
- Play golf
- Assign tasks to the firm secretary (may be business-value-added)
- Fill out time sheets for client work (is business-value-added)

c.   A large law firm probably has paralegals and associates to perform some of the above-mentioned tasks as well as other non-value-added activities that were not mentioned. For instance, there may be someone in a large firm to drive the lawyers to court so that they can use the time for other value-added activities.

Exercise 5
a.   None of the items are value-added activities; products should be designed so that schedule changes are not needed.

b.   The cost driver is number of factory schedule changes.

c.   The plant manager needs to do a better job of planning so that factory schedule changes are eliminated except those requested by a customer (who should then be charged for the cost of the change) or those that are necessary for significant quality improvements and cost reductions.

Exercise 7
Each student will have different answers. No solution is provided.

Exercise 9
a.   Receiving ingredients (NVA)   45
       Moving ingredients to stockroom (NVA)   15
       Storing ingredients in stockroom (NVA)   7,200
       Moving ingredients from stockroom (NVA)   15
       Mixing ingredients (VA)   50
       Cooking ingredients (VA)   185
       Bottling ingredients (VA)   90
       Moving bottled chowder to warehouse (NVA)   20
       Storing bottled chowder in warehouse (NVA)   10,080
       Moving bottled chowder from warehouse to trucks (NVA)   30

b.   Cycle time = 45 + 15 + 7,200 + 15 + 50 + 185 + 90 + 20 + 10,080 + 30 = <u>17,730</u>

       MCE = (50 + 185 + 90) ÷ 17,730 = 0.018

c.   Mr. Brady might consider a just-in-time inventory purchasing and production system. His longest times are in storage on the front and back end of the production process and in moving the goods in and out of storage. He also may want to negotiate some long-term contracts with his customers so that he has a better idea of when they will want what quantities of his chowder.

Exercise 11
a.   number of pizzas cooked
b.   number of deliveries made, number of kilometres driven, age of vehicles
c.   age of building, type of construction, square metres
d.   number of side orders, proportion of number of pizzas
e.   value of building, location of building, square metres of building
f.   number of kilometres driven, average kilometres per hour

Exercise 13
a.   Cost of printing books at a publishing house (B or U)
b.   Cost of preparing payroll cheques (O)
c.   Cost of supplies used in research and development on an existing product (P)
d.   Salary of the Vice-President of Marketing (O)
e.   Cost of developing an engineering change order (P)
f.   Depreciation on camera at Drivers' License Office in the Department of Motor Vehicles (P)
g.   Salary of guard for 5-story headquarters building (O)
h.   Cost of paper and cover for a passport (U)

Exercise 15
a. $450,000 \div 150,000$ calls = $3 per call
       $150,000 \div 10,000$ purchase orders = $15 per purchase order
       $110,250 \div 7,000$ receiving reports = $15.75 per receiving report

       Cost assignment:

118 calls X $3	$ 354
37 purchase orders X $15	555
28 receiving reports X $15.75	441
Total	$1,350

b. $1,350 \div 200$ units = <u>$6.75</u> per unit

c. $3 X 0.75 = $2.25 per call
       $15 X 0.75 = $11.25 per purchase order
       $15.75 X 0.75 = $11.81 per receiving report

       Cost assignment:

20 calls X $2.25	$ 45.00
15 purchase orders X $11.25	168.75
8 receiving reports X $11.81	94.48
Total	$308.23 ÷ 200 = <u>$1.54</u>

Exercise 17.
a.   Overhead: $13,200,000 ÷ 55,000 DLHs = $240 per DLH

	Plastic Bottles	**Control Panels**
Revenue	$6,000,000	$13,000,000
Direct material	(1,360,000)	(1,200,000)
Direct labour	(28,000)	(742,000)
Overhead	[a] (480,000)	[b] (12,720,000)
Profit (loss)	$4,132,000	$(1,662,000)

[a] $240 x 2,000 = $480,000
[b] $240 x 53,000 = $12,720,000

b.   Overhead: $13,200,000 ÷ 206,250 MHs = $64 per MH

	Plastic Bottles	**Control Panels**
Revenue	$ 6,000,000	$13,000,000
Direct material	(1,360,000)	(1,200,000)
Direct labour	(28,000)	(742,000)
Overhead	[a] (7,680,000)	[b] (5,520,000)
Profit (loss)	$(3,068,000)	$5,538,000

[a] $64 x 120,000 = $7,680,000

[b] $64 x 86,250 = $5,520,000

c.   Overhead:
        $9,500,000 ÷ 55,000 DLHs = $173 per DLH
        $2,500,000 ÷ 206,250 MHs = $12 per MH
        $1,200,000 ÷ $19,000,000 = $0.06 per revenue $

	Plastic Bottles	**Control Panels**
Revenue	$6,000,000	$13,000,000
Direct material	(1,360,000)	(1,200,000)
Direct labour	(28,000)	(742,000)
Overhead	[a](2,146,000)	[b](10,984,000)
Profit	$2,466,000	$ 74,000

[a]
($173 x 2,000) + ($12 x 120,000) + ($.06 x $6,000,000)
= $346,000 + $1,440,000 + $360,000 = $2,146,000

[b]
($173 x 53,000) + ($12 x 86,250) + ($0.06 x $13,000,000)
= $9,169,000 + $1,035,000 + $780,000 = $10,984,000

d.   Overhead: $9,500,000 ÷ 55,000 DLHs = $173 per DLH
$2,500,000 ÷ 206,250 MHs = $12 per MH

	Plastic Bottles	**Control Panels**	**Total**
Revenue	$6,000,000	$13,000,000	$19,000,000
DM	(1,360,000)	(1,200,000)	(2,560,000)
DL	(28,000)	(742,000)	(770,000)
OH	[a](1,786,000)	[b](10,204,000)	(11,990,000)
Profit	$2,826,000	$ 854,000	$ 3,680,000
Admin. OH			(1,200,000)
Profit			$ 2,480,000

[a]
($173 x 2,000) + ($12 x 120,000) = $346,000 +
$1,440,000 = $1,786,000

[b]
($173 x 53,000) + ($12 x 86,250) = $9,169,000 +
$1,035,000 = $10,204,000

e.   The solution in Part d best reflects the profit generated by each product because overhead costs are assigned using a related cost driver. Neither product is burdened with overhead truly caused by the other. And, unless there is some cause-effect relationship between administrative overhead costs and revenue dollars, it is best to deduct these from total company income.

PROBLEMS

Problem 1

a.   The production process in this company has a significant amount of non-value-added time built into the lead time. The most likely cause of this NVA time is one or more bottleneck processes that create long wait periods when no production is occurring and goods are simply stored or stacked until they can pass through the process.

A fairly simple way to determine where the bottlenecks are is to walk through the plant and see where materials or partially completed units are being stacked in sight or are being brought back into the production area from a storage location. Another indicator of a bottleneck is where labour is waiting on a machine to complete a process so that additional materials can be added.

In addition to bottlenecks, the company could be engaging in rush orders that remove regularly scheduled production from processing. Always trying to catch up on back orders will create delays in processing current orders. It is possible that if all back orders were filled, the current orders could be processed at a much more rapid pace. Finally, defective units caused by rushing to complete orders will have to be reworked, thereby causing an even longer delay in processing time.

b.   A value chart could be developed that would identify all of the activities associated with the production and sale of nameplate stands. The value chart would identify what is occurring with the nameplates during the entire cycle time. The value chart would identify for management the areas of operation that need to be improved to reduce cycle time. It would also be used by management to reduce costs by reducing or eliminating non-value-added activities.

Problem 3

Salary for receiving clerks = \$28,000 ÷ 240 days = \$117 per day
Salary for quality personnel = \$40,000 ÷ 240 days = \$167 per day
Salary for handling personnel = \$19,000 ÷ 240 days = \$79 per day
Salary for setup personnel = \$26,000 ÷ 240 days = \$108 per day
Building costs = (\$125,000 + \$35,000) ÷ 365 days = \$438 per day;
\$438 ÷ 100,000 square metres = \$0.004 per square metre per day

Cost for receiving personnel (1.5 x 117)	$ 176
Cost for quality personnel (5 x $167)	835
Cost for handling personnel (3 x $79)	237
Cost for setup personnel (1 x $108)	108
Cost of storage (500 sq. metres x $0.004 x 37.5 days)	75
Cost of waiting (10 x $50)	500
Cost of shipping delay (2.5 x $50 x 500)	62,500
Total cost	$64,431
Divided by number of units	÷ 500
Total cost of NVA activities per unit	$ 129

Problem 5

a.   Base wages: $63,000,000 ÷ 3,150,000 = $20 per DLH
Health care[1]: $10,500,000 ÷ 2,100 = $5,000 per worker
Payroll taxes: $5,040,000 ÷ $71,700,000 = $0.07 per dollar
Overtime: $8,700,000 ÷ 12,000,000 = $0.725 per unit
Training: $1,875,000 ÷ 300 = $6,250 per new hire
Retirement: $6,900,000 ÷ 2,100 = $3,286 per worker
Workers' Safety & Insurance: $1,200,000 ÷ 2,100 = $571 per worker

b.   Although more labour-related items are driven by the number of factory workers, the number of regular labour hours accounts for the most labour cost ($63,000,000).

c.   It can be inferred that the use of overtime hours minimizes some cost drivers. In this example, use of overtime hours would help contain health care costs, training costs, retirement costs and workers' safety and insurance costs.

[1] Depending upon the province, solutions in parts a and c will differ.

Problem 7

a.   Professional salaries: $900,000 ÷ 30,000 = $30 per hour
Building costs: $450,000 ÷ 15,000 = $30 per square metre
Risk management: $320,000 ÷ 1,000 = $320 per patient

b.   Surgery = (6,000 X $30) + (1,200 X $30) + (200 x $320) = $280,000
Inpatient care = (20,000 x $30) + (12,000 x $30) + (500 x $320) = $1,120,000
Outpatient Care = (4,000 x $30) + (1,800 x $30) + (300 x $320) = $270,000

c.   Surgery: professional hours (this activity base would drive many costs related to surgery and would be easy to track)
In-patient care: days in hospital (this activity base would be easy to follow and would account for use of time and space)

Outpatient care: professional hours (this activity base would capture service provision to outpatients); or expected patient volume (this activity base would capture those costs that are more related to capacity to provide service)

Problem 9

a.   Allocation rates:

Utilities ($487,500 ÷ 65,000) $7.50 per MH
Scheduling & setup ($273,000 ÷ 780) $350 per setup
Materials handling ($640,000 ÷ 1,600,000) $0.40 per kilogram
Building depreciation ($457,600 ÷ 35,200) $13 per sq. metre

	Product A	Product B	Product C
Direct costs	$ 40,000	$ 65,000	$ 90,000
Utilities	262,500	75,000	150,000
Scheduling & setup	45,500	133,000	94,500
Material handling	200,000	120,000	320,000
Building depreciation	156,000	107,900	193,700
Total	$704,000	$500,900	$848,200
Units produced	63,000	10,000	40,000
Cost per unit	$ 11.17	$ 50.09	$ 21.21

b.   Overhead rate: ($487,500 + $273,000 + $640,000 + $457,600) ÷ (32,000 + 18,000 + 50,000) = $1,858,100 ÷ 100,000 = $18.581

	Product A	Product B	Product C
Direct costs	$ 40,000	$ 65,000	$ 90,000
Overhead	594,592	334,458	929,050
Total	$634,592	$399,458	$1,019,050
Units produced	63,000	10,000	40,000
Cost per unit	$ 10.07	$ 39.95	$ 25.48

c.   ABC pricing:
Product A: $11.17 x 1.20 = $13.40
Product B: $50.09 x 1.20 = $60.11
Product C: $21.21 x 1.20 = $25.45

Pre-ABC pricing:
Product A: $10.07 x 1.20 = $12.08
Product B: $39.95 x 1.20 = $47.94
Product C: $25.48 x 1.20 = $30.58

d.   The conventional approach to product costing used only one allocation base, direct labour hours which was unable to fully capture the causes of overhead cost incurrence. The ABC approach provided better overhead allocation because of the superior relationship between the cost pools and the cost drivers used to allocate the overhead cost. (It be noted that ABC is more expensive to use than the conventional approach.)

To the extent that there is an error in determining cost, prices will also be in error if they are based on costs as is evident in this problem. Although Product A is relatively unaffected by the choice of costing system, Products B and C have substantially different costs and prices under the two systems. The traditional costing system would result in underpricing Product B and overpricing Product C which could affect both sales volume and company profitability.

Problem 11

a.

Fax stands ($4 x 100,000)	$ 400,000
Organizers ($30 x 10,000)	300,000
Printer stands ($10 x 30,000)	300,000
Total	$1,000,000

b.   Allocation rates:
Quality control: $50,000 ÷ 140,000 = $0.36 per unit (100,000; 10,000; 30,000)
Setup: $50,000 ÷ 500 = $100 per setup (100; 200; 200)
Material handling: $150,000 ÷ 1,000,000 = $0.15 per kilo (200,000; 500,000; 300,000)
Equipment operation: $750,000 ÷ 500,000 = $1.50 per MH (100,000; 200,000; 200,000)

Cost allocation:

	Fax	Organizers	Printers
Quality control	$ 36,000	$ 3,600	$ 10,800
Setups	10,000	20,000	20,000
Material handling	30,000	75,000	45,000
Equipment operation	150,000	300,000	300,000
Total	$226,000	$398,600	$375,800
Divided by number of units	÷ 100,000	÷10,000	÷ 30,000
Overhead cost per unit	$ 2.26	$ 39.86	$ 12.53

Cost per unit:

	Fax	Organizers	Printers
DM	$ 4.00	$15.00	$ 8.00
DL	6.00	18.30	9.00
OH	2.26	39.86	12.53
Total	$12.26	$73.16	$29.53

c.   Relative to the prices developed based on the costs of the products found using activity based costing, costs under the traditional costing system would generate higher prices for fax stands and lower prices for the other two products.

Problem 13

a.   1.   Obtain the existing cost information and reports on the accounts receivable department.

The purpose of the department is to collect receivables from the customers. The budget of the department is $22,500,000.

2.   Determine the major processes that occur within the accounts receivable department.

Observations, interviews, storyboards, and analyses of company records could identify the processes of the department.

3.   Identify the inputs that start each process and the outputs that each process produces.

4.   Determine the activities in the process.

5.   Identify the resources used by each activity.

6.   Define an output measure, financial or nonfinancial, for each major activity.

7.   Define a performance measure, financial or nonfinancial, for each major activity.

8.   Record the actual performance on the selected performance measures.

9.   Compare the actual performance measure to historical performance, an external benchmark, or a target.

10.   Find improvement ideas.

b.   Factors that Canada Hydro's top management should consider before carrying out an activity-based analysis of the accounts receivable department include the following:

- Activity-based analysis can be very expensive.
- Results can lead to recommendations that, if implemented, will bring significant changes within the organization.
- These changes will affect employees and there could be some resistance.
- Management should plan the implementation carefully to minimize problems.
- Management must be very supportive and willing to commit the time, financial resources, and human resources that will ensure the success of the project.

Problem 15

a.   Overhead rate: $900,000) 150,000 machine hours = $6 per machine hour

Bid price per unit of job #287	
Direct materials	$0.35
Direct labour	0.85
Applied overhead [(1,500 machine hrs. x $6/hr) ÷ 6,000 units]	1.50
Full manufacturing cost per unit	$2.70
Mark-up (0.25 x $2.70)	0.68
Bid price per unit	$3.38

b.   Activity rates

Purchasing and receiving materials	$200,000 ÷ 2,500 purchases & receiving	$80
Machine operating costs	$450,000 ÷ 150,000 MH	$3 per MH
Materials handling	$80,000 ÷ 400,000 material moves	$0.20/move
Shipping	$170,000 ÷ 300,000 kilometres	$0.57/kilometre

Bid price per unit of #287

Direct materials	$0.35
Direct labour	0.85
Activities:	
Purchasing and receiving materials	
[($80 x 2 purchases & receipts) ÷ 6,000 units]	0.03
Machine operating costs [($3 x 1,500 machine hours) ÷ 6,000 units	0.75
Materials handling [($0.20 x 300 moves) ÷ 6,000 units]	0.01
Shipping [($0.57 x 2,300 kilometres) ÷ 6,000 units]	0.22
	$2.21
Mark-up (0.25 x $2.21)	0.55
Bid price per unit	$2.76

Using an activity-based approach, Mars Company's bid price of $2.76 per unit is lower than Arrow Company's bid price of $2.95 per unit. Thus, Mars is more likely to receive the contract.

Alternative solution:

Bid price per unit of job #287

Direct materials (6,000 x $0.35)	$ 2,100
Direct labour (6,000 x $0.85)	5,100
Activities	
Purchasing and receiving materials ($80 x 2 purchases & receipts)	160
Machine operating costs ($3 x 1,500 machine hours)	4,500
Materials handling ($0.20 x 300 moves)	60
Shipping ($0.57 x 2,300 kilometres)	1,311
Full manufacturing costs	$13,231
Full manufacturing costs per unit ($13,231 ÷ 6,000 units)	$ 2.21
Mark-up (0.25 x $2.21)	0.55
Bid price per unit	$ 2.76

Problems 13 & 15 are adapted by the authors from *Management Accounting Examinations*, published by the Certified General Accountants Association of Canada © CGA-Canada, 1999 (15) and 2000 (#13), used by permission.

CHAPTER 7
RELEVANT COSTING

QUESTIONS

1.   For a cost to be relevant it must be associated with the decision; it must differ between alternatives; and its incurrence must be in the future. If any of these factors are not true, the cost is not relevant and will not impact the firm's performance between choices of alternatives.

4.   At the time when Bill must make his decision as to whether he will attend the concert, the original cost of $50 paid by Jim, and the price paid by Bill, $25, both represent sunk costs. They are therefore irrelevant. The only relevant cost is the $30 opportunity cost which represents the price Ted is willing to pay for the ticket.

   He will incur a $30 opportunity cost. The opportunity cost represents the benefit he will sacrifice (i.e., $30 of revenue) to attend the concert.

6.   All historical costs are called sunk costs. Such costs are never relevant to a decision, as these costs do not differ between alternatives.

8.   The relevant cost would be the incremental or avoidable costs. They would include: a, c, and d. Items b and e are not relevant because they both involve historical costs (irrelevant sunk costs).

10.   Yes. Any incremental fixed costs would be relevant. For example, there could be fixed costs for a production set-up that would be relevant, or the required purchase of a new machine.

12.   The relevant factors would include: a, b, d, and e. All of these items would have an impact on profitability. The only item that would not be relevant would be the fixed production costs which are volume independent within the relevant range.

15.   The compensation structure is the primary incentive that management can control to direct the efforts of sales personnel. By manipulating the compensation structure, management can induce sales people to focus on certain product lines, certain geographical markets, or specific customers.

17.   The statement is true if "incremental costs" include any opportunity costs
        associated with dedication of company resources to this special order. For
        example, if a company were operating at full capacity and wanted to bid on a
        special order, the bid price would also have to include the contribution margin on
        the displaced product sales that would be made if the special order were not
        undertaken.

19.   Some fixed costs can be traced directly to a product line, but the discontinuation
        of the product line would not result in termination of the cost. Examples of such
        costs would include the salaries of managers who could not be dismissed if the
        product line were terminated, and the depreciation charges associated with
        production equipment for which there is no alternative use.

EXERCISES
Exercise 1
a.   Incremental revenue:
                Product AA: ($1.50 - $1.00) x 10,000 = $5,000
                Product BB: ($3.00 - $0.50) x 20,000 = $50,000
                Product CC: ($0.90 - $0.75) x 500 = $75

                Incremental costs:
                Product AA: $0.75 x 10,000 = $7,500
                Product BB: $1.00 x 20,000 = $20,000
                Product CC: $0.10 x 500 = $50

b.   Incremental profit
                Product AA: $5,000 - $7,500 = $(2,500)
                Product BB: $50,000 - $20,000 = $30,000
                Product CC: $75 - $50 = $25

Product AA should not be further processed because the incremental revenue from the additional processing will not cover the costs of the additional processing. Product BB should be further processed because doing so generates incremental profits. Product CC generates incremental profit. However, due to the very small incremental benefit, the company may choose not to process CC further.

Exercise 3
Income from reworking the product:

Sales		$20,500
Cost of rework	12,500	
Selling costs (3% of sales)	615	13,115
		$ 7,385
Income from selling scrap parts:		
Sales		$ 6,850

The Chow-Chow bottles should be reworked because the company will receive $535 more by reworking the product than it would by selling the bottles for scrap.

Exercise 5
a.   The incremental cost of the new truck is:

Purchase price:	$ 10,000
Less salvage on the old truck	5,000
Incremental purchase cost	$ 5,000

b.   Incremental savings on operating the new truck:

Operating costs of the old truck	$ 6,000
Operating costs of the new truck	4,500
Incremental operating savings	$ 1,500

c.   To make this decision, one can simply compute the total incremental savings
        (over the three year life of the trucks) if the new truck is purchased, and
        compare such savings to the costs of purchase.

Incremental savings on operating the new truck (from part b) (1,500 X 3 years)	4,500
Purchase cost of new truck (from part a):	(5,000)
Incremental net cost	(500)

The company is $500 better off if it keeps the old truck.

Exercise 8

a.

	Make	Outsource (Buy)
Variable costs:		
$3 x 20,000	$ 60,000	
$5 x 20,000		$100,000
Fixed costs	50,000	0
Total relevant costs	$ 110,000	$100,000

The firm would be $10,000 per year better off to outsource (buy) the
pumps rather than make them.

b.

	Make	Outsource (Buy)
Variable costs:		
$3 x 30,000	$ 90,000	
$5 x 30,000		$ 150,000
Fixed costs	50,000	0
Total relevant costs	$ 140,000	$ 150,000

The firm would be better off by $10,000 in making the pumps rather than
outsourcing (buying) them.

c.   Let x equal the volume of pumps required for production. Then the cost to make
        the pumps equals $50,000 + $3x$ and the cost to buy the pumps equals $0 + $5x$.
        To find the point of indifference, set the two equations equal to each other:

$50,000 + $3x = $5x$
$x = 25,000$ units

Exercise 10

a.

	Sanders	Drills
Sales price (per unit)	$45	$ 28
Variable costs	30	19
CM	$15	$ 9
Divide by required machine hrs.	÷ 8	÷ 6
CM per machine hour	$1.88	$ 1.50

Because the sanders generate more CM per MH than drills, the company should make only sanders:

Total hours ÷ hours per unit = units produced
     90,000 ÷ 8 = <u>11,250</u> sanders

b.   [(11,250 ✱ $15) - $110,000] = <u>$58,750</u>

Exercise 12

a.

	Grooming	Training	Total
Revenue	$150,000		$150,000
10,000 X $15		$200,000	200,000
8,000 X $25			
Variable Costs:			
Labour:			
10,000 X $5	(50,000)		(50,000)
8,000 X $10		(80,000)	(80,000)
Materials:			
10,000 X $1	(10,000)		(10,000)
8,000 X $2		(16,000)	(16,000)
Contribution Margin	$90,000	$104,000	$194,000
Fixed Costs	(100,000)	(90,000)	(190,000)
Net Income	$(10,000)	$ 14,000	$ 4,000

b.   Contribution Margin ratios:
       Grooming: $90,000 ÷ $150,000 = 0.60
       Training: $104,000 ÷ $200,000 = 0.52

       The additional $1 should advertise Grooming services. For Grooming, each additional dollar of revenue generates $0.60 of CM; for Training only $0.52 of CM is generated from each dollar of sales.

c.   Each billable hour of Grooming service generates $9 of contribution margin ($15 - $5 - $1), and an hour of Training services generates $13 of contribution margin ($25 - $10 - $2). The advertising should therefore be spent on the Training service.

Exercise 14
a.   SP(X) = FC + VC(x) + NIBT; X = 18,000 sets
      $200 X 18,000 = $1,100,000 + ($20 + $30 + $40 + $10) X 18,000 + NIBT
      $3,600,000 = $1,100,000 + $1,800,000 + NIBT
      NIBT = $3,600,000 - $2,900,000 = $700,000

b.   New VC = $100 - $10 + $2 = $92;
      New CM $170 - $92 = $78 on 5,000 sets.
      Sets sold at old CM = 15,000
      ($100 X 15,000) + ($78 X 5,000) = $1,100,000 + NIBT
      $1,500,000 + $390,000 - $1,100,000 = NIBT = $790,000

      Yes, since income would increase by $90,000, it should accept the offer.

c.   Sean Graham Company would need to quote a selling price high enough to
      cover its variable costs of production ($92), to cover the current loss of $100,000
      ($100 X 10,000 = $1,000,000 of CM minus $1,100,000 of FC), and earn the profit
      of $150,000.

Cost of production	$ 92
Coverage of loss ($100,000 ÷ 5,000)	20 — *amount /unit to cover loss*
Generation of income ($150,000 ÷ 5,000)	30 — *profit per unit*
Total selling price	$ 142

Exercise 16
a.   Contribution of special order
      50,000 * [$21.50 - ($18 + $1)] $ 125,000
      Loss of regular sales

Beginning Inventory	$ 10,000		
Production	320,000		
Goods available	$ 330,000		
Special order	50,000		
	$ 280,000		
Expected regular sales	300,000		
Lost sales	$ 20,000		
Less: 40% recovery	8,000		
Net loss	$ 12,000	x $9	108,000

      Difference $ 17,000

      The order should be accepted since the contribution to fixed costs is greater.

b.   They could lower the price by $17,000 ÷ 50,000 = $0.34 to $21.16 so as not to
      lose or gain.

c.   i.   Will this offer have any backlash effect on present customers?
     ii. Are more orders expected from this customer who would negate the 40% recovery of lost sales?
     iii. Is this the kind of customer we wish to deal with?
     iv. Accuracy of estimates (demand, recovery, etc.)
     v.   Effect on other future sales.

Exercise 19

a.   Selling price = incremental cost of production + commission
     SP = $0.45 + 0.10SP
     SP = $0.50
     1,000 x 0.50 = $500 bid price

b.   SP = $0.45 + 0.10SP + 0.10SP
     SP = $0.5625; 1,000 x $0.5625 = $562.50 bid price

c.   SP = $0.45 + ($200 ÷ 1,000) + 0.10SP +0.05SP
     SP = $0.65 + 0.15SP
     SP = $0.76471 = $764.71 bid price

Exercise 20

a.   The effect of the change on overall net income can be found by analyzing sales and avoidable expenses:

Sales	$ 250,000
Variable costs:	
Professional services	150,000
Marketing	37,500
Contribution margin	$ 62,500
Avoidable direct fixed costs	35,000
Product margin	$ 27,500

Overall net income would decline by an amount equal to the Product margin, $27,500, if the After-Dinner segment was eliminated.

b.   Some of the more important qualitative factors to be considered would include: the effect of the elimination of the After-Dinner segment on business in the other two segments, prospects for long-term increases in business volume in the After-Dinner segment, the effect on the company and its employees in closing down a segment, and what kind of alternative managerial actions might be successful in turning the segment around.

PROBLEMS

Problem 1

Sales (Product C) 800 X $10	$	8,000
Sales (Product D) 1,200 x $20		24,000
Total final sales value	$	32,000
Sales value at end of process 1		18,000
Incremental revenue	$	14,000
Incremental costs		16,000
Incremental profit	$	(2,000)

The incremental processing (process 2) should not have been done. It generates an incremental loss of $2,000.

Problem 3

a.

	Aferon		Beteron		Ceteron	
Sales value after processing		$ 520		$ 350		$ 265
Less:						
Value at split-off point	$450		$300		$ 250	
Processing cost	38	488	55	355	18	268
Incremental profit (loss)		$ 32 [1]		$ (5) [2]		$ (3) [3]

Based on the above analysis, Aferon is the only product that should be processed further, since it is the only one that enjoys an incremental profit after further processing.

In answering this part of the question, it is also necessary to determine if Losell would be better off if they were to discontinue production entirely.

The relevant revenues and incremental costs to be considered are the incremental revenues of processing Aferon. The incremental processing losses on Beteron and Ceteron are not relevant since the above analysis shows that they should be sold at the split-off point rather than being processed further. However, the revenues to be derived from Beteron and Ceteron at the split-off point are relevant since, in order to produce Aferon, Beteron and Ceteron will also be produced.

Consequently, the relevant revenue and incremental costs are:

	Processed Aferon	Unprocessed Beteron	Unprocessed Ceteron	Total
Revenues	$520	$300	$250	$1,070
Incremental separate cost	38			38
Incremental gross contribution	$482	$300	$250	$1,032
Incremental joint costs				850
Incremental profits				$ 182

Recommendation: Losell should continue the joint process but should sell Beteron and Ceteron at the split-off point. Aferon should be processed further and then sold. This combination would result in the greatest profitability to Losell.

Alternative Method: [1] Aferon = $450 - $520 = $70 - $38 = $32; [2] Beteron = $300 - $350 = $50 - $55 = ($5); [3] Ceteron = $250 - $265 = $15 - $18 = ($3)

b.   Since Deteron will not be produced if this opportunity is declined, the incremental cost of producing Deteron must be included in the evaluation of the proposal.

Incremental revenues ($400 - $250)		$150
Incremental costs:		
Separate process Ceteron	$18	
Cost of modifying Ceteron to Deteron	140	158
Incremental loss		$ 8

Losell should not produce Deteron.

Extract from *Management Accounting Examinations*, published by the Certified General Accountants Association of Canada (© CGA-Canada, 1995). Reprinted by permission.

Problem 5
<u>Current system</u>

Spoilage cost: 5,000,000) 200 = 25,000	
Lost variable costs 25,000 x $17.50	$ 437,500
Inspection cost $0.10 x 5,025,000	502,500
External failure cost	
i. Replacement of products	
5,000,000) 500 = 10,000 x $17.50	175,000
ii. Lost customers (potential)	
5 x 10,000 x ($33.00 - $17.50 - $4.95[1])	<u>527,500</u>

[1] 15% of $33.00

Annual cost of spoilage (including opportunity cost)	<u>**$1,642,500**</u>
Lease cost of new system	$ 200,000
Spoilage cost: 5,000,000 ÷ 350 = 14,286 x $17.50	250,005
Inspection cost $0.065 x 5,014,286	325,929
External failure cost	
i. Replacement of products	
5,000,000 ÷ 900 = 5,556 x $17.50	97,230
ii. Lost customers (potential)	
5 x 5,556 x ($33.00 - $17.50 - $0.035[1] - $4.95)	<u>292,107</u>
	<u>$ 1,165,271</u>

[1] Reduction in variable cost of inspection $0.10 - $0.065

Therefore, the new system saves in the cost of quality $1,642,500 - $1,165,271 = $477,229.

Extract from *Management Accounting Examinations*, published by the Certified General Accountants Association of Canada (© CGA-Canada 1993). Reprinted by permission.

Problem 10
a.   Relevant costs of making:

Salaries and wages (avoidable)	$ 1,950,000
Office supplies	350,000
Occupancy costs	300,000
Selling and Administration	450,000
Total	$ 3,050,000

Relevant cost of outsourcing (buying):

Price from trucking firm	$ 2,500,000
Salaries and wages	150,000
Materials	100,000
Occupancy costs	300,000
Office supplies	50,000
Selling and Administration	56,000
Total	$ 3,156,000

Advantage of making: $3,156,000 - $3,050,000 = $106,000

b.   Some of the concerns other managers might have include

- how the cost shifted from the Distribution Department will affect the evaluations of their departments,
- how the transfer of personnel will affect their operations,
- what the behavioural implications might be of shifting personnel and their responsibilities,
- how reliable the freight company is relative to the Distribution department, and
- whether the new arrangement creates any new managerial responsibilities.

(IMA adapted)

Problem 13

a.   The rationing decision should be based on a comparison of the contribution margin that can be generated from each product per unit (minute, hour, or day) of oven time:

	Birthday Cakes	Wedding Cakes	Special Occasion Cakes
Sales	$25	$100	$40
Variable Costs			
Direct materials	5	30	10
Direct labour	5	15	8
Variable overhead	2	5	4
Variable selling	3	12	5
Contribution Margin	$10	$38	$13
Required oven time	10 min.	80 min.	18 min.
Contribution margin per minute of oven time	$1	$0.475	$0.722

Since the birthday cakes generate the highest contribution margin per minute of oven time, and given the fact that demand for birthday cakes is high enough to consume all of the oven's available time, only birthday cakes should be produced. This use of the oven will maximize company profit.

b.   Total available oven time in minutes = 690 hrs x 60 mins = 41,400. According to the conclusion in part a., only birthday cakes will be produced.

Production in units: 41,400 ÷ 10 = 4,140 birthday cakes

Sales (4,140 x $25)	$ 103,500
Variable costs:	
Direct materials (4,140 x $5)	20,700
Direct labour (4,140 x $5)	20,700
Variable overhead (4,140 X $2)	8,280
Variable selling (4,140 X $3)	12,420
Contribution margin	$ 41,400
Fixed costs:	
Manufacturing costs	1,200
Selling and administrative	800
Operating income	$ 39,400

c.   The marketing manager needs to be sensitive to how the seasons affect the demand for the company's products. For example, since demand is much higher during the holiday season, the marketing manager needs to be focused on selling the mix of products that will maximize the firm's contribution margin.

Alternatively, during other seasons when demand is slack, the marketing manager simply needs to concentrate on promoting all products; capacity constraints will not be a consideration. Since virtually all fixed costs are irrelevant in the short-term, the marketing manager should be willing to accept all orders that generate a positive contribution margin. The marketing manager must also bear in mind the loss of repeat business if customers are turned away.

Problem 14

a.

	Hot Dogs		
	No Action	**Strategy 1**	**Strategy 2**
Sales	$150,000	$141,000	$165,000
Direct materials	40,000	37,600	44,000
Direct labour	15,000	14,100	16,500
Commissions	0	0	10,450
Fixed costs	45,000	45,000	45,000
Net Profit	$50,000	$44,300	$49,050

	Burgers		
	No Action	**Strategy 1**	**Strategy 2**
Sales	$125,000	$180,000	$156,250
Direct materials	55,000	79,200	68,750
Direct labour	10,000	14,400	12,500
Commissions	0	0	7,500
Fixed costs	15,000	44,000	15,000
Net Profit	$45,000	$42,400	$52,500
Total Profits	$95,000	$86,700	$101,550

To maximize profits, Victor should implement strategy number 2. It would increase profits by $101,550 - $95,000 = $6,550.

b.   Victor should consider behavioural effects of both employees and customers. For customers, Victor should be confident that sales efforts of employees can shift the product mix. If Victor's assumptions are incorrect in this regard, he may add a sales commission, for example, and find that although total sales rise, the percentage of burgers sold remains as before. With regard to employees, Victor needs to make certain that the employees will find a 10% commission to be a salient incentive. Otherwise, total costs will rise but total sales may remain flat.

Problem 19

a.

	Shirts	Hats	Boots	Total
Revenue	$110,000	$60,000	$35,000	$205,000
Variable costs				
Raw Material.	(15,000)	(22,000)	(13,000)	(50,000)
Direct Labour	(27,000)	(10,000)	(10,000)	(47,000)
Overhead	(6,000)	(4,250)	(3,500)	(13,750)
Selling &Administrative	(16,000)	(5,000)	(6,000)	(27,000)
Contribution Margin	$46,000	$18,750	$2,500	$67,250
Fixed Production				(14,750)
Selling and Administration				(20,700)
Operating Profit				$31,800

The boots product line should be retained because it contributes $2,500 to overall profits of the company.

b.   In the role of marketing manager, you might be concerned about how the elimination of one product line would affect sale of other lines. For example, although boots may not be very profitable as a product line, they may serve to draw customers into the store to purchase shirts and hats. This may indicate that some sales of other product lines are dependent on the availability of the boot line.

Problem 22

	Sticky Notes	Tablets	Custom Stationery
Sales	$800,000	400,000	$1,000,000
Variable costs:			
Production	200,000	150,000	550,000
Selling	150,000	100,000	200,000
Contribution Margin	$450,000	$150,000	250,000
Direct fixed Costs*			
Production	14,545	7,273	118,182
Selling	109,091	14,545	66,364
Product Margin	326,364	128,182	65,454
Production	145,455	72,727	181,818
Selling	90,909	45,455	113,636
NIBT	$ 90,000	$ 10,000	$(230,000)

(handwritten margin notes): } direct fixed. } unavoidable fixed cost

Based on the product margin (sales less all direct and avoidable costs), all product lines should be retained. If the custom stationery product line were dropped, overall corporate profits would decline by approximately $65,454.

*   Computation of direct and allocated fixed costs:

Computation of allocated fixed costs

Production:
Sticky Notes: $400,000 x ($800,000) $2,200,000) $ 145,455
Tablets: $400,000 x ($400,000) $2,200,000)   72,727
Cust. Stat. $400,000 x ($1,000,000) $2,200,000)   181,818
Total $ 400,000

Selling:
Sticky Notes: $250,000 x ($800,000) $2,200,000) $ 90,909
Tablets: $250,000 x ($400,000) $2,200,000)   45,455
Cust. Stat.: $250,000 x ($1,000,000) $2,200,000)   113,636
Total $ 250,000

Computation of direct fixed costs

	Production	**Selling**
Total fixed cost: Sticky Notes	$160,000	$ 200,000
Total allocated fixed cost	145,455	90,909
Direct fixed costs	$14,545	$ 109,091
Total fixed cost: Tablets	$ 80,000	$ 60,000
Total allocated fixed cost	72,727	45,455
Direct fixed costs	$ 7,273	$ 14,545
Total fixed cost: Custom Stationery	$ 300,000	$ 180,000
Total allocated fixed cost	181,818	113,636
Direct fixed cost	$ 118,182	$ 66,364

CHAPTER 8
CONTROLLING COSTS

QUESTIONS

1. Cost control for any event is exerted before, during, and after that event. Control is exerted before the event to determine the expected cost and to provide a plan to achieve the expected cost. During an event, control is exerted so that the cost is incurred at the planned level. After an event, actual and planned performance are compared and explanations of differences are developed. By understanding why differences exist, managers can act to minimize future negative differences between the actual and planned amounts or to change processes so that positive differences can be maintained.

3. On-the-job training helps instill cost consciousness in employees by making employees aware of the significance of cost control. Training employees to perform their jobs correctly will tend to make employees recognize when processes could be performed better and often at less cost. Cost control suggestions should be encouraged and rewarded by employers. Also, training is an effective investment in human resources because workers can apply the concepts and skills they are learning directly to the jobs they are performing.

5. Companies can (a) pass along the costs as price increases to maintain the same income level; (b) decrease other costs to maintain the same income level; or (c) experience a decline in net income. Possibility (a) may not be an option if prices are highly fixed by competitive market forces, unless all firms in the industry respond in the same manner to the increased costs. Possibility (c) is generally unacceptable from any stakeholder point of view. Thus, the most rational way to cope with increased costs in an area over which little control can be effected is to try and better control costs in areas over which managers and employees have the most control.

7. A items are those having the highest dollar volume; these are likely to be some of the most expensive parts and materials used in production. C items are those having the lowest dollar volume; these are likely to be parts and materials that are used in small volume or are of very low value on a per unit basis. B items are those that fall between A and C items; they have moderate dollar volume.

9. In the not-too-distant past the decision on sourcing would have been based almost exclusively on price. Although price is still a significant factor in the decision, today, companies are more likely to place weight on the ability of the supplier to deliver reliable, high-quality goods. The nature of the relationship has also changed to allow for more cooperation between customer and supplier. Both the supplier and the customer realize that their mutual survival depends on jointly reducing costs and delivering greater value to the customer. To facilitate this type of communication and cooperation, firms are reducing the number of suppliers they purchase from and are attempting to purchase more standardized parts.

11. One reason might be that total cost does not significantly change over a wide range of order quantities around the EOQ. Another reason is that the EOQ does not consider the relationship of the particular item to the production requirements of other items. Finally, the EOQ does not consider capacity (e.g., storage space) available.

12. JIT views inventory as a liability because it costs the company money to hold inventory. Inventory represents an investment for which there is no current demand. JIT works at streamlining operations so that carrying inventory is unnecessary.

15. Time, space, and energy all have associated costs. Increasing throughput, minimizing the time from receiving customer orders to delivery of the product results in lower costs. Eliminating production and storage space minimizes unnecessary movements (energy) during production, and reduces the tendency to allow inventory to sit idly (time) in storage thereby reducing inventory carrying costs. Rearranging production facilities minimizes unnecessary movements (energy) and improves production flow (time and energy). Aiming for zero defects reduces rework (time and energy) costs by doing things right the first time.

16. Research shows that 80–90 percent of a product's life-cycle cost is determined during the development stage. Also, these decisions affect product sales, design, and quality.

18. The life-cycle stage is important because it determines the types of costs that are incurred. For example, early in the life cycle, costs are incurred for research and development, process design, market research, and building prototypes. Later in the life cycle, costs are incurred for actually making the product, and distributing and marketing the product. By understanding the product life cycle, managers can concentrate cost management efforts on the activities that are associated with each stage of the life cycle.

20. A cross-functional team can benefit from the diverse sets of knowledge possessed by team members. Perspectives from finance, engineering, marketing, production, and product design can be given simultaneously in developing the product. The benefit of this approach is that all the organizational consequences of alternative designs can be evaluated effectively.

    Alternatively, an engineering team, which certainly would have depth of knowledge in product and process design, would not have the breadth of knowledge to evaluate new products from multiple perspectives. As a result, the different organizational effects of alternative product designs would not be evaluated as effectively as would be possible with a cross-functional team.

EXERCISES

Exercise 1.
a. Cost understanding
b. Cost containment
c. Cost avoidance or cost containment
d. Cost reduction or cost avoidance
e. Cost avoidance (long-term; discuss, however, the significant costs incurred to effect this move)
f. Cost understanding
g. Cost reduction or cost avoidance

Exercise 3
a. 6
b. 4
c. 1
d. 2
e. 8
f. 5
g. 7
h. 9
i. 3

Exercise 5
a. N
b. C
c. C
d. C
e. O
f. O
g. C
h. N/A
i. O
j. C
k. N
l. N
m. O
n. C
o. N/A

Exercise 7

$EOQ = \sqrt{[(2QO) \div C]}$

a. $EOQ = \sqrt{[(2 \times 8{,}100 \times \$1) \div \$2]}$
        $= \underline{90}$

b. $40 = \sqrt{[(2 \times Q \times \$2) \div \$4]}$
        $1{,}600 = (\$4 \times Q) \div \$4$
        $\$6{,}400 = \$4 \times Q$
        $\underline{1{,}600} = Q$

c. $100 = \sqrt{[(2 \times 1{,}000 \times \$15) \div C]}$
        $10{,}000 = \$30{,}000 \div C$
        $C = \underline{\$3}$

d. $20 = \sqrt{[(2 \times 400 \times \$5) \div C]}$
        $400 = \$4{,}000 \div C$
        $C = \underline{\$10}$

e. $30 = \sqrt{[(2 \times 150 \times O) \div \$3]}$
        $900 = (300 \times O) \div \$3$
        $\$2{,}700 = 300 \times O$
        $O = \underline{\$9}$

Exercise 9.
a. $EOQ = \sqrt{[(2 \times 7{,}300 \times \$.75) \div \$.48]}$
        $= \underline{151}$ kilograms.

b.   Daily usage = $7{,}300 \div 365 = 20$ kilograms per day
        Order point = $20 \times 18 = \underline{360}$ kilograms;

c.   Safety stock = $20 \times 3 = 60$ kilograms

d. $20 \times 0.1 \times 18 = 36$ kilograms

e.   For maximum usage over lead time:
        $(0.1 \times 20$ kgs$)(18$ days $+ 3$ days$)$ 42
        For normal usage in extra 3 days(20×3) $\underline{60}$
        Total safety stock   102
        Normal usage during lead time $\underline{360}$
        Order point $\underline{462}$ kilograms

PROBLEMS

Problem 1

This exercise is intended to evoke student thought. Many different answers can be expected. The following answers are provided as an example of an employer's perspective:

	Potential Advantages	**Potential Disadvantages**
a.	Less expensive, more flexible;	Less control; more errors in work, less reliable
b.	Lower cost	Less reliable; less flexible
c.	Less expensive, more flexible; recruiting technique for checking out potential full-timers	Lower quality; poor preparation; less control; lower reliability
d.	Less expensive, more flexible; quicker service; recruiting technique checking out potential full-timers	Lower quality; less reliable
e.	Less expensive; more flexible	Risk of theft; poor public relations; poor service
f.	Lower cost; obtain less experienced people	Less committed employees; less effective because employee probably has a full-time job elsewhere
g.	Less expensive; more flexible	Less reliable; less control; poor-quality work
h.	Less expensive; more flexible	Lower quality credentials; lower quality delivery; not available outside class
i.	Less expensive; more flexible	Less control over doctors; less loyalty; lower quality of services
j.	Less expensive; more flexible	Less control over writing quality

Problem 3

a. Only the costs that would actually vary over the short run with the number of orders placed would be considered:

Cost per order for supplies	$0.95
Phone expense	3.20
Total	$4.15

b. Only the costs that would actually vary in the short run with the quantity of materials stored would be considered:

Insurance premium	$0.15
Obsolescence cost	0.12
Total	$0.27

Problem 5

a. Case A

$$400 = (20 \times 12) + SS$$
$$SS = \underline{160}$$

Case B

$$OP = (30 \times 10) + 60$$
$$= \underline{360}$$

Case C

$$120 = (DU \times 7) + 50$$
$$70 = DU \times 7$$
$$DU = \underline{10}$$

Case D

$$300 = (15 \times LT) + 30$$
$$270 = 15 \times LT$$
$$LT = \underline{18}$$

Case E

$$500 = (DU \times 5) + 60$$
$$440 = DU \times 5$$
$$DU = \underline{88}$$

Problem 7
a. JP
b. PD
c. PSR&D
d. PP
e. PL
f. PSR&D
g. PL
h. JP
i. AI
j. AI
k. PP
l. PL
m. PP
n. PL
o. PD
p. JP
q. PD

CHAPTER 9
THE BUDGETING PROCESS

QUESTIONS

1.   Budgeting has significant advantages in improving communications, motivation, coordination and teamwork. It allows management to visualize the future state of affairs in time to make adjustments in order to effect more desirable results. It is a major tool in planning and controlling. The more complex and diversified the company, and the greater the degree of competitive intensity it faces, the more important budgeting is.

The basic budgeting process begins with planning. Planning involves the setting of objectives and translating those objectives into required activities and needed resources. The process also includes a control function of measuring whether the predetermined objectives have been successfully attained and providing feedback to concerned and involved parties. Setting objectives and translating them into required activities and needed resources are the most important steps.

Imposed budgets are appropriate:
- In start-up stages of a business
- In very small businesses
- In businesses facing economic crisis
- Where subordinates lack budgetary skills
- Where organizations require precise coordination of effort

All of these settings call for strong control by top management.

4.   Budget slack is the intentional understatement of revenue or overstatement of budgetary expense. Slack allows subordinates to achieve contrived expectations with less effort than if they had no slack built in. To reduce the occurrence of slack, operating managers can be rewarded with bonuses for budgeting relatively high performance levels and achieving those levels.

6.   Cost variances should be based on actual volume rather than budgeted volume because variable costs change with changes in volume. Accordingly, as sales volume changes, total variable cost also changes. Thus, to evaluate cost control, costs must be compared to a budget that is based on the same volume as actual volume.

7.   A continuous budget is one developed in which management adds a new month 12 months into the future as the current month expires. This process is thought to be less disruptive than the traditional process. When continuous budgeting is used, the budgeting process occurs throughout the year rather than in a specific period of each year.

9.   It is said to be a static budget because it is based on a single level of demand. It must be static to facilitate the many time-consuming financial arrangements that must be made before beginning operations for the budget year, based on planned (or budgeted) volumes.

11.   The master budget is driven entirely by expected sales. Sales drive production needs, which drive materials purchasing, labour and overhead costs, cash payments, etc. Expected sales also drive cash collections on sales, so are a very important component of the cash budget.

13.   The materials purchases budget is driven by the production budget and the firm's inventory policies with respect to materials. Since materials are required for production to commence, the amount of materials acquired in a particular period will reflect the production budget for that period. However, the material purchases budget will not be strictly proportional to production if the firm desires to increase or decrease its level of materials inventory.

15.   Managers must control cash in order to be able to pay the company's obligations when due. The cash budget is essential in control of cash in terms of: (1) cash available exclusive of financing, (2) cash excess/inadequacy, (3) cash available/needed, and (4) financing options for acquisition of needed cash or disposition of unneeded cash.

        Managers estimate collections from sales through historical company data on collection patterns, industry trends/patterns, and judgment. Current economic information can play an important part in estimating the collection pattern since inflation/deflation, interest rates, and employment affect both businesses' and consumers' abilities to pay. Cash collections are important in the budgeting process because of their impact on the cash budget and the availability of funds with which to make disbursements for operating expenditures, capital expenditures, and ownership distributions.

16.   A firm's credit policies significantly affect the cash collection pattern. Liberal credit terms allow customers to pay at some point in the future without incurring substantial interest costs. Alternatively, a tight credit policy is designed to encourage credit-sale customers to pay early. The cash collection pattern is further influenced by policies regarding which customers should be granted credit. If risky customers are granted too much credit, uncollectible accounts will rise. If less risky customers are denied credit, total sales and cash collections will decline.   A firm gives a discount to encourage customers to pay for their purchases early.

A company might wish to maintain a minimum cash balance because of the uncertainty in the budgetary process or to have funds on hand in the event of an emergency. If cash collections are slower or cash disbursements are higher than expected, the minimum cash balance provides a cushion or margin of safety to fall back on. It is also possible that the company's bank requires a minimum cash balance in the corporate account as either a condition of the account or as a compensating balance for an outstanding loan.

18.   The spreadsheet program allows managers to do "what if" analyses. This type of analysis allows the management team to evaluate the effects of errors in their estimates or possible changes in the plans. By linking the various budgets in the spreadsheet, a change can be made in one variable and its effects will automatically flow through all affected budgets. For example, the sales estimates could be changed and the impact of the sales change on all budgets would be shown immediately.

19.   Zero-based budgeting, ZBB, is a process that considers priorities for activities and alternatives for achieving current and proposed activities in relationship to company objectives. Managers must annually (or periodically) evaluate which of the ongoing activities should be continued, eliminated, or funded at a lower level. Government settings have historically engendered a phenomenon known as empire building whereby bureaucrats ask for successively larger budget appropriations. ZBB is an antidote for empire building. Managers are consistently required to justify proposed spending, so ZBB is a good fit with government departments.

EXERCISES

Exercise 1

a.   5
b.   6
c.   7
d.   3
e.   4
f.   2
g.   1
h.   9
i.   8

Exercise 4

$38 x 206,000	$40 x 206,000	$40 x 200,000
$7,828,000	$8,240,000	$8,000,000

|_____| |_____|
        Sales price variance   Sales volume variance

        $412,000 U $240,000 F
        |_____|
            Total variance = $172,000 U

Because the company sold a greater number of units than was planned (6,000 units), at the standard price of $40, $240,000 of additional revenues were generated (as measured by the sales volume variance). Unfortunately, this was more than offset by an unfavourable sales price variance resulting from actual sales being made at an average of $2 per unit less than planned. This $2 shortage, multiplied by the 206,000 actual units sold resulted in an unfavourable price variance of $412,000. The two variances ($240,000 F + $412,000 U) explain the total revenue shortfall of $172,000.

Exercise 6

a.   Expected revenue = (1.20 x 30 x $4,000) = <u>$144,000</u>

b.

$3,500 x 39	$4,000 x 39	$4,000 x 36
$136,500	$156,000	$144,000

|_____| |_____|
        Sales price variance   Sales volume variance

        $19,500 U $12,000 F
        |_____|
            Total variance = $7,500 U

The favourable variance caused by giving three extra seminars was more than offset by a lower-than-budgeted seminar fee.

Exercise 8
a.

	Quarter				
	1st	**2nd**	**3rd**	**4th**	**Total**
Sales	200,000	150,000	250,000	180,000	780,000
+ Desired end. bal.*	60,000	100,000	72,000	88,000	88,000
= Total needed	260,000	250,000	322,000	268,000	868,000
− Beg. balance**	80,000	60,000	100,000	72,000	80,000
= Production	180,000	190,000	222,000	196,000	788,000

* Forty percent of subsequent quarter's sales.
** Forty percent of current quarter's sales.

b.   There are costs associated with carrying finished goods inventory. For example, costs include obsolescence, insurance, storage, security, and theft loss. By reducing the level of finished goods inventory, these costs would also be reduced.

Exercise 10
a. and b.

	Production
Sales	74,000
+ Desired ending balance	6,300
= Total needed	80,300
- Beginning balance	4,000
= Units to produce	76,300

	Purchases in Kilograms	
	A	**B**
Needed for production	152,600$^{(1)}$	381,500$^{(2)}$
+ Desired ending balance	4,900	6,000
= Total needed	157,500	387,500
- Beginning balance	4,000	6,100
= Kilos to be purchased	153,500	381,400
Purchases cost	$736,800$^{(3)}$	$800,940$^{(4)}$

$^{(1)}$ (76,300 x 2) = 152,600
$^{(2)}$ (76,300 x 5) = 381,500
$^{(3)}$ (153,500 x $4.80) = $736,800
$^{(4)}$ (381,400 x $2.10) = $800,940

c.   Improved materials management could reduce the level of raw material inventory carried. One way to improve management of materials would be to adopt JIT inventory management. As inventory levels are reduced, the firm can expect to lower the costs of obsolescence, spoilage, theft, insurance, handling, and warehousing.

Exercise 12

a.

Collections for	April	May	June	Discounts Memo
April from February	$ 17,640[1]			
April from March	64,960[2]			
April from April:				
Cash sales	74,400[3]			
Credit	85,064[4]			$1,736[5]
May from March		$ 16,240		
May from April		69,440		
May from May:				
Cash sales		87,600		
Credit		100,156		2,044
June from April			$ 17,360	
June from May			81,760	
June from June:				
Cash sales			81,600	
Credit			93,296	1,904
Totals	$242,064	$273,436	$274,016	$ 5,684

[1] $252,000 x 0.7 x 0.1
[2] $232,000 x 0.7 x 0.4
[3] $248,000 x 0.3
[4] $248,000 x 0.7 x 0.5 x 0.98
[5] $248,000 x 0.7 x 0.5 x 0.02

b.

Accounts Receivable	
Apr. 1 98,840	
248,000	242,064
292,000	1,736
272,000	273,436
	2,044
	274,016
	1,904
115,640	

Proof:

	50% of June credit sales	$ 95,200
	10% of May credit sales	20,440
	Total	$115,640

Alternative solution to Exercise 12. This assumes that cash sales receive the same discount as the credit sales that are paid in the month of purchase.

a.

Collections for	April	May	June	Discounts Memo
April from February	$ 17,640[1]			
April from March	64,960[2]			
April from April:				
Cash sales	72,912[3]			
Credit	85,064[4]			$3,224[5]
May from March		$ 16,240		
May from April		69,440		
May from May:				
Cash sales		85,848		
Credit		100,156		3,796
June from April			$ 17,360	
June from May			79,968	
June from June:				
Cash sales			81,600	
Credit			93,296	3,536
Totals	$240,576	$271,684	$272,384	$10,556

[1] $252,000 x 0.7 x 0.1
[2] $232,000 x 0.7 x 0.4
[3] $248,000 x 0.3 x 0.98
[4] $248,000 x 0.7 x 0.5 x 0.98
[5] [$248,000 x (0.3 + (0.7 x 0.5)] x 0.02

b.

Accounts Receivable	
Apr. 1 98,840	
248,000	240,576
292,000	3,224
272,000	271,684
	3,796
	272,384
	10,556
115,640	

Proof:	50% of June credit sales	$ 95,200
	10% of May credit sales	20,440
	Total	$115,640

Exercise 14

a.   Collections in March:

January (0.14 x $400,000)	$ 56,000
February (0.60 x $300,000)	180,000
March (0.22 x $360,000)	79,200
Total	$315,200

b.   The best way to reduce uncollectible accounts is to better screen customers in approving credit sales. By granting credit only to less risky customers, the level of bad debts will be reduced. A second approach would be to adopt a more aggressive collection policy for delinquent accounts. This might involve a collection agency or involvement of the legal department.

Exercise 17

Bold Enterprises
Cash Budget
For 2008

Beginning cash balance		$ 10,000
Collections from sales and on account		468,600
Cash available exclusive of financing		$478,600
Disbursements		
Payments on account --operations & purchases	$ 90,000	
Direct labour	100,000	
Overhead	127,000	
SG&A	93,000	
Total planned disbursements		410,000
Cash excess or (inadequacy)		$ 68,600
Minimum cash balance desired		4,000
Cash available or (needed)		$ 64,600
Financing		
Borrowings (repayments)	$(45,600)	
Liquidate (acquire) plant assets	(14,800)	
Receive (pay) interest	(4,200)	
Total impact of financing		(64,600)
Ending cash balance		$ 4,000

PROBLEMS

Problem 1
a.   2, 3 & 5
b.   1 & 4
c.   1, 2 ,3 ,4 & 6
d.   2, 3 & 5
e.   1 & 7
f.   5 & 8
g.   1 & 5
h.   1, 2, 3, 5, 6 & 8

Problem 4

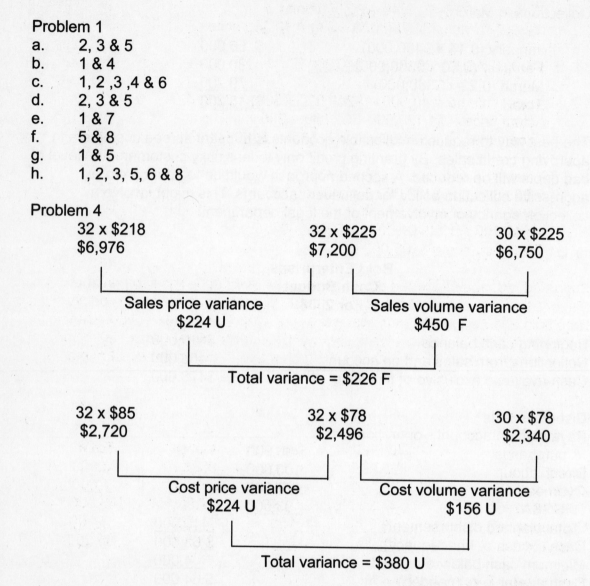

| 32 x $218 | 32 x $225 | 30 x $225 |
| $6,976 | $7,200 | $6,750 |

Sales price variance
$224 U

Sales volume variance
$450 F

Total variance = $226 F

| 32 x $85 | 32 x $78 | 30 x $78 |
| $2,720 | $2,496 | $2,340 |

Cost price variance
$224 U

Cost volume variance
$156 U

Total variance = $380 U

There is a favourable volume variance. At standard price and cost, his favourable net difference ascribed to volume is $294 ($450 - $156). However, this advantage was more than offset by the fact that he charged less and the costs (cost price) he incurred were higher than expected. The combined unfavourable price variances amount to $448 ($224 U + $224 U). His shortfall of $154 ($4,410 - $4,256) can be explained as follows:

Amount due to volume at standard prices	$294 F
Amount due to price difference	448 U
Net difference	$154 U

Problem 6

a.   Pucks: $800,000 ÷ $40 = 20,000 units
       Shoulder Pads: $1,200,000 ÷ $30 = 40,000 units

b. $40 X (21,000 - 20,000) = $40,000 F

c.   Actual volume = 40,000 - ($240,000 ÷ $30) = 32,000
       Actual price = $1,120,000 ÷ 32,000 = $35
       Price variance = 32,000 X ($30 - $35) = $160,000 F

d.   Total price variance
       = $63,000 U + $160,000 F = $ 97,000 F
       Total volume variance
       = $40,000 F + $240,000 U = $200,000 U
       Total variance = $103,000 U

Budgeted revenue exceeded actual revenue by $103,000. The two principal reasons that actual revenue was lower than budgeted revenue are (1) pucks were sold at a lower price than budgeted and (2) too few shoulder pads were sold. These negative effects were partially, but not completely, offset by (1) a higher price for shoulder pads and (2) a higher-than-planned sales volume of pucks.

Problem 10
Production

	January	February	March	Total
Sales	36,000	32,000	30,000	98,000
Desired ending balance	8,000	7,500	7,000	7,000
Total needed	44,000	39,500	37,000	105,000
Estimated beg. balance	9,000	8,000	7,500	9,000
Production	35,000	31,500	29,500	96,000

Purchases   Direct   Material M

	January	February	March	Total
Production (times 3)	105,000	94,500	88,500	288,000
Desired ending balance	6,000	5,625	5,250	5,250
Total needed	111,000	100,125	93,750	293,250
Estimated beg. balance	6,750	6,000	5,625	6,750
Purchases in kilograms	104,250	94,125	88,125	286,500

Purchases- Direct Material N

	January	February	March	Total
Production (times 2)	70,000	63,000	59,000	192,000
Desired ending balance	4,000	3,750	3,500	3,500
Total needed	74,000	66,750	62,500	195,500
Estimated beg. balance	4,500	4,000	3,750	4,500
Purchases in kilograms	69,500	62,750	58,750	191,000

Purchases - Direct Material O

	January	February	March	Total
Production (times 4)	140,000	126,000	118,000	384,000
Desired ending balance	8,000	7,500	7,000	7,000
Total needed	148,000	133,500	125,000	391,000
Estimated beg. balance	9,000	8,000	7,500	9,000
Purchases in kilograms	139,000	125,500	117,500	382,000

b.   The nature of the production process affects the efficiency of the conversion of materials into finished products. One of the benefits of utilizing higher technology is the reduction that can be achieved in waste, scrap, and defective products. It may be expected that the materials required per unit of finished products will drop to some extent if the new technology is acquired, and also that there will be an increase in capacity (production) and possibly an increase in sales.

c.   The vendor of the new technology, an in-house engineering department, and knowledgeable production managers should be able to offer valuable insights as to how material requirements will change with acquisition of the machine technology. In fact, the change in material requirements is likely to have been one of the factors that were considered in evaluating the purchase of the new technology.

Problem 12

a.   Sales ($420,000 ÷ 0.65) $646,154
       CGS   (65%) $420,000
       GM   (35%) $226,154

b. $420,000 - $24,000 = Variable CGS
       $396,000 = Variable CGS

       Total variable cost = 0.70 x $646,154 = $452,308
       Variable SGA = Total Variable Cost - Variable CGS
       = $452,308 - $396,000 = $56,308

c.   Net income   = 0.15 x Sales = 0.15 x $646,154 = $96,923
       Total fixed costs = Sales - Total variable costs - Net income
       = $646,154 - $452,308 - $96,923 = $96,923

d.   Cash collections in June for June = 0.75 x $646,154   = <u>$484,616</u>
       Cash payments in June for June
       = 0.60 (Total Variable Cost + Total Fixed Cost - Depreciation)
       = 0.60 x ($452,308 + $96,923 - $7,000) = <u>$325,339</u>

Problem 14

a.   May cash collections:

From April	$144,400
From May revenue ($360,000 x 0.60)	<u>216,000</u>
Total May collections	<u>$360,400</u>

b.   May 31 inventory balance:

Beginning inventory	$108,000
Purchases [0.75(0.60 x $360,000)]	
+ [0.75 (0.40 x $480,000)]	<u>306,000</u>
Total available	$414,000
CGS (0.75 x $360,000)	<u>270,000</u>
Ending inventory	<u>$144,000</u>

c.   May 31 retained earnings balance:

Beginning balance (May 1, 2008)	$220,400
Add net income*	<u>34,800</u>
Ending balance	<u>$255,200</u>

*Net income:	
Sales	$360,000
CGS (75% of sales)	<u>270,000</u>
Gross margin	$ 90,000
Operating exp. [$48,000 + (0.02 x $360,000)]	<u>55,200</u>
Net income	<u>$ 34,800</u>

d.

May beginning cash balance	$ 40,000
May collections	<u>360,400</u>
Total available exclusive of financing	$400,400
Disbursements:	
Accounts payable	$272,000
Other ($48,000 - $2,000)	<u>46,000</u>
Total planned disbursements	<u>318,000</u>
Cash excess or (inadequacy)	$ 82,400
Minimum cash balance desired	<u>40,000</u>
Cash available or (needed)	$ 42,400
Financing:	
Borrowings (repayments)	$ 0
Liquidate (acquire) assets	<u>0</u>
Total impact of planned financing	<u>0</u>
Ending cash balance	<u>$ 82,400</u>

e.   A minimum cash balance protects the firm from errors in its projections regarding cash payments or receipts and allows the firm a cushion in case unexpected developments occur. Further, the firm's bank may require the minimum balance as a condition of a loan.

Problem 16

a.   Accounts receivable at July 31:

no discount

75% of July's sales (0.75 x $92,000)	$69,000
15% of June's sales (0.15 x $102,000)	15,300
Balance	$84,300

there only this much left for sun

_____ Accounts payable at July 31
(0.40 x July purchases of $58,000) $23,200

b.   Cash collections expected in August from:

June sales (0.15 x $102,000)	$ 15,300
July sales (0.60 x $92,000)	55,200
August sales (0.25 x $116,000)	29,000
Total	$99,500

c.   Cash disbursements expected in August:

A/P from July 31	$ 23,200.00
Purchases of August (0.98 x 0.60 x $79,600)	46,804.80
Subtotal	$ 70,004.80
Other [$24,000 + (0.12 X $116,000)]	37,920.00
Total	$107,924.80

d.

Baldwin's Fresh Fruit Stand
Cash Budget
For August 2008

Beginning August balance*	$ 28,000.00
Cash collections in August	99,500.00
Total available exclusive of financing	$127,500.00
Disbursements	107,924.80
Cash excess or (inadequacy)	$ 19,575.20
Minimum cash balance desired	28,000.00
Cash available or (needed)	$ (8,424.80)
Financing:	
Borrowing (repayment)	$ 8,424.80
Liquidate (acquire) investments	0.00
Total impact of planned financing	$ 8,424.80
Ending cash balance	$ 28,000.00

*Cash flow in the months of May, June and July are sufficiently negative that the beginning balance in August is the minimum cash balance, $28,000.

e.

Baldwin's Fresh Fruit Stand
Income Statement
For August 2008

Sales		$116,000
Cost of goods sold (60%)		69,600
Gross margin (40%)		$ 46,400
Operating expenses		
Depreciation	$ 4,000	
Other expenses	37,920	41,920
Net income before taxes		$ 4,480

f. For perishable commodities, the threat of spoilage is much more significant than that for more durable materials. Consequently, there must be a much tighter match between production and sales than for other products. This almost mandates the use of JIT to manage the level of inventories.

Problem 19

a. Cash collections from sales:

Q1	($400,000 x 45%)	$180,000
Q2	($400,000 x 50%)	200,000
		$380,000

Cash disbursements for purchases:
Purchases:

for Q2 sales ($400,000 x 40%)	$160,000
for Q3 sales ($800,000 x 25% x 40%)	80,000
Less: Opening inventory in Q2 ($400,000 x 25% x 40%)	(40,000)
	$200,000

Cash disbursements

for Q1 purchases ($200,000 x 0.5)	$100,000
for Q2 purchases ($200,000 x 0.5)	100,000
	$200,000

Other cash expenditures:

Manufacturing overhead	$ 10,000
Payroll	30,000
Selling costs	8,000
Administration costs	10,000
Dividends	20,000
Total	$ 78,000

Josh Lyman Co.
Cash Budget for Q2, 2008

Cash on hand at April 1, 2008		$ 25,000
Plus: cash receipts from sales		380,000
		$405,000
Less: Cash disbursements:		
Purchases	$200,000	
Other	78,000	278,000
Cash on hand at July 31, 2008		$127,000

b. Advantages of budgeting include the following:
- Aids planning by helping management identify problems before they occur
- Compatible with management by exception
- Communicates top management's plans and goals
- Compatible with management by objectives
- Aids subsequent performance evaluation
- Brings planning to the forefront
- Provides a means of allocating resources within the firm

Extract from *Management Accounting Examinations*, published by the Certified General Accountants
tion of Canada (© CGA-Canada 2000). Reprinted with permission.

CHAPTER 10
RESPONSIBILITY ACCOUNTING AND TRANSFER PRICING
IN DECENTRALIZED ORGANIZATIONS

QUESTIONS

1.   In centrally organized firms, decision making is concentrated among a few individuals—those at the top of the organizational hierarchy. In decentralized firms, the authority and responsibility for making decisions is pushed down to lower level managers. The rationale is that lower level managers have more information about their areas of the business and are in the best position to make decisions for those areas.

3.   While many skills are common to managers in centralized and decentralized firms, the decentralized manager must be willing to accept greater risk. The greater risk is associated with a performance evaluation that is based on the results achieved rather than the managerial actions taken. The managers must accept the authority to make decisions, execute the decisions, and live with the outcome. This requires the decentralized manager to be creative, goal-oriented, assertive, and decisive.

5.   The costs may include the costs of poor decisions by inexperienced managers; the costs associated with a divergence between organizational, organizational segment, and individual goals (these are sometimes called agency costs or costs of suboptimization); the costs of duplicating activities across subunits; the costs of a more sophisticated planning and communication network; the costs of a more sophisticated accounting system; and the costs of training new managers.

7.   A segment manager should be evaluated only on factors (costs and revenues) that are directly traceable to his/her segment <u>and</u> under his/her control. Alternatively, the segment should be evaluated on all factors that are directly traceable to the segment *and* necessary for the segment's operation. These two sets of factors are not completely overlapping. For example, the salary of the segment manager can be traced to the segment (and is therefore used to evaluate the segment), but it is not controllable by the segment manager (and therefore is not used to evaluate the segment manager).

9.   In the broadest sense, a variance is a deviation between a planned outcome and an actual outcome. By focusing managerial attention on variances, the factors that generate a difference between the desired result and actual result can be identified. Once the causal factors are recognized, managers can take actions to exploit favourable factors and overcome unfavourable factors. Such actions should bring a closer alignment between planned and actual results.

11.   Suboptimization occurs when the goals of the individual manager, his/her subunit, and the organization are not in harmony. Generally, suboptimization occurs because subunit managers are too focused on maximizing the performance of their subunits rather than maximizing the performance of the overall organization. In turn, this result is often caused by inappropriate incentive contracting systems (performance-based pay systems).

13.   Transfer prices are internally set (agreed upon) prices with which a selling division transfers goods or services to a buying division. The role of the transfer price is to provide goal congruence while retaining subunit autonomy, and provide motivation for managers to be effective and efficient in their operations.

15.   Standard costs have the advantage of being known or agreed upon in advance and of being a measure of efficient production. Actual costs may vary widely from month to month because of large changes in production volume, seasonal variations, and efficiencies.

17.   Dual pricing is the permitting of the selling division to record one transfer price (higher) and the buying division to record another (lower). This practice is intended to minimize suboptimization and create goal-congruent incentives for both divisions.

19.   Because transfer prices between multinational units of a company can affect profits and inventory values reported in two different countries, managers must be cognizant of setting prices, within legal and ethical limits, to minimize income taxes and tariffs.

EXERCISES

Exercise 1
a.   4
b.   5
c.   10
d.   6
e.   7
f.   1
g.   3
h.   2
i.   9
j.   8

Exercise 3
a.   D
b.   A
c.   A
d.   D
e.   D
f.   A
g.   A
h.   A
i.   A
j.   N

Exercise 5
a.   Price variance =
(Actual price - Expected price) x Actual Sales volumes
= ($ 39.50 - $42.00) x 425,000
= $1,062,500 U

Volume variance =
Projected price x (Actual volume - Projected volume)
= $42 x (425,000 - 410,000)
= $630,000 F

b.   A sales mix variance can be computed only in firms that sell more than one product; this is a single-product company.

c.   No, a determination cannot be made as to whether profits were above or below estimated levels. Information on costs would be required to make that determination.

Exercise 7

a., b., c., d

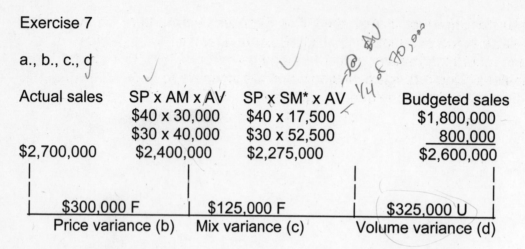

Actual sales	SP x AM x AV	SP x SM* x AV	Budgeted sales
	$40 x 30,000	$40 x 17,500	$1,800,000
	$30 x 40,000	$30 x 52,500	800,000
$2,700,000	$2,400,000	$2,275,000	$2,600,000

$300,000 F	$125,000 F	$325,000 U
Price variance (b)	Mix variance (c)	Volume variance (d)

(a) Total variance = $2,700,000 - $2,600,000 = $100,000 F
*SM = 25% shoes, 75% baseball gloves

Exercise 9

a. The upper limit for the transfer is the lowest outside price at which the buying division can purchase a comparable water pump: $55. The lower limit is the relevant cost to produce and sell the unit: $20.40 + $4.20 + $12.60 = $37.20.

b. $48

c. $48 - $10.80 = $37.20

d. This would be a breakeven price for the Accessory Division. It would have an incentive to make the transfer only if its profits could be increased by doing so.

Exercise 11

a. Units sold internally = $75,000 ÷ $1.25 = 60,000 units
Total production = 60,000 ÷ .4 = 150,000 units
External sales = 150,000 - 60,000 = 90,000 units
Internal variable costs = $30,000 ÷ 60,000 = $.50 per unit
External variable costs = $45,000 ÷ 90,000 = $.50 per unit
External sales price = $135,000 ÷ 90,000 = $1.50 per unit
Change in gross profit = ($1.40 - $1.25) x 60,000
= $9,000

b. ($1.25 - $1.70) x 60,000 = $(27,000)

c. Transfer price = $1.25 + ($.15 ÷ 2)
= $1.325 per unit

d.   A dual transfer price would allow the Office Supplies Division to record the internal sales at the external price of $1.40 per unit, and allow the Garden Division to record the transfer at the existing internal price, $1.25 per unit. The dual transfer pricing arrangement would provide incentive to both the buying and selling divisions to make the internal transfer.

Exercise 13
a.   A
b.   D
c.   A
d.   D
e.   A
f.   D
g.   A
h.   A
i.   D

PROBLEMS

Problem 1
a.   The most significant problem is that the variances are computed by comparing the static budget to the actual expenses. To evaluate cost control, a flexible budget should be compiled at the actual level of activity. Variances should be computed by comparing the flexible budget to actual costs. An additional weakness is that the performance evaluation does not contain auxiliary performance measures including measures of product quality and customer service.

b.

	Flexible Budget	Actual	Variance
Activity level	$1,800,000	$1,800,000	$ 0
Variable Costs:			
Professional labour	$900,000	$940,000	$40,000 U
Travel	45,000	40,000	5,000 F
Supplies	90,000	90,000	0
Fixed Costs:			
Professional labour	400,000	405,000	5,000 U
Facilities cost	250,000	265,000	15,000 U
Insurance	80,000	78,000	2,000 F
Totals	$1,765,000	$1,818,000	$53,000 U

c.   The variances that are most likely to be investigated are the ones that are material and may be attributed to controllable factors. The most material variances are for the variable cost of professional labour (4.44% over the flexible budget), travel (11.11% under the flexible budget), and the facilities cost (6% over budget).

d.   Upper management should establish the criteria that determine which variances are to be investigated. They should be assisted in this task by managerial accountants.

Problem 3

a.

	Actual	Standard	Variance
Metal	$507,500	$420,000	$87,500 U
Galvanizing	65,800	70,000	4,200 F
Direct labour	104,300	105,000	700 F
Overhead			
Welding supplies	34,900	31,500	3,400 U
Utilities	38,300	38,500	200 F
Indirect labour	25,500	28,000	2,500 F
Machine M/R	21,200	14,000	7,200 U
Equip. depr.	77,000	77,000	0
Miscellaneous	29,500	28,000	1,500 U
	$904,000	$812,000	$92,000 U

b.   Overall, Ms. Padgett generated $92,000 of costs in excess of the budget. However, much of the excess cost may have been beyond her control. For example, the most significant variance is for metal. Based on the preceding analysis, it is not possible to determine whether that variance is due to a price or quantity factor. If the variance for metal is largely comprised of a price variance, it is unlikely that Ms. Padgett has control over price. This variance should be used to evaluate the purchasing department. This is true of all other inputs as well. As a production supervisor, Ms. Padgett would be responsible for the quantity of inputs used but would not have control over the price of inputs used. Consequently, the variance for each item should be decomposed into a price and quantity element.

The variances that would likely be investigated would include metal, galvanizing, and maintenance/repair. The key criteria to decide which variances are worthy of investigation are controllability and magnitude. It makes no difference if the variance is favourable or unfavourable.

Problem 5

a.

Revenues		$80,000
Variable expenses		
Meals and lodging	$36,000	
Supplies	2,000	38,000
Contribution margin		$42,000
Fixed expenses		
Speakers	$10,000	
Rent on facilities	7,200	
Advertising	4,200	21,400
Controllable segment margin		$20,600
Allocated fixed costs		5,000
Profit		$15,600

b.

Revenues		$77,000
Variable expenses		
Meals and lodging	$43,200	
Supplies	2,400	45,600
Contribution margin		$31,400
Fixed expenses		
Speakers	$15,500	
Rent on facilities	8,400	
Advertising	5,800	29,700
Controllable segment margin		$ 1,700
Allocated fixed costs		5,000
Profit		$(3,300)

c.

Revenues	$ 3,000 U
Meals & Lodging	7,200 U
Supplies	400 U
Contribution margin	$10,600 U
Rent on facilities	1,200 U
Advertising	1,600 U
Speakers	5,500 U
Controllable segment margin	$18,900 U
Allocated fixed costs	0
Profit	$18,900 U

The factors most responsible for the difference between budgeted and actual profit of the tax seminar are the volume of participants and the failure to budget for the airline costs of the speakers. The extra volume of participants, in turn, is related to the additional advertising and the reduction in the seminar fee.

d.   It is fortunate for Professor Thomas that he is already tenured. Virtually all of the difference between actual and budgeted profit from the seminar can be attributed to actions taken by Professor Thomas. In addition to the mistake (omission of $5,000 for transporting speakers), Professor Thomas demonstrated a lack of knowledge of cost causality. By lowering the seminar fee, Professor Thomas pushed volume up sufficiently to cause certain fixed costs to rise (advertising, and rent on facilities). It doesn't appear that Professor Thomas was effective in managing the relationship between costs and activities.

Problem 7

a.

- Current external selling price $5,400
  Selling Division--fair value since most are produced
  and sold at this price externally. Buying Division--price is higher
  than what could be purchased elsewhere so this would make its performance
  report appear worse than by buying externally.

- Total variable production cost ($2,100)+ 20% = $2,520
  Selling Division--contributes minimally to covering
  fixed costs and therefore no profit is shown from
  these sales as opposed to external sales. There is little incentive to sell
  internally if the selling division can sell all its output externally.
  Buying Division--less than external purchase price; therefore, it is
  more beneficial to the bottom line of Heavy-Duty Equipment.

- Total product ($3,000) cost + 20% = $3,600
  Selling Division--covers some but not all costs for this division; therefore,
  incentive to sell internally isn't there if Motor Division can
  sell its output externally.
  Buying Division--purchase price below external, which is better for margin in
  this division.

- Bid price from external supplier ($4,800)
  Selling Division--allows for some profit which is an incentive to sell internally
  unless it can sell all its output externally.
  Buying Division--no incentive to buy internally since it costs the same to buy
  from an external supplier.

b.   Upper limit = $4,800
      Lower limit = costs of $2,400 + contribution margin of $3,000 = $5,400
      Since the lower limit exceeds the upper limit, the company would be better off not
      making the internal transfers.

Problem 9

a.   (000's)

	Bottle	Perfume	Irresistible Scents
Revenue (6,000)	$ 20,000	$ 127,800	$ 127,800
Cost	(14,400)	(116,780)	(111,180)
Margin	$ 5,600	$ 11,020	$ 16,620
Return on sales	28%	8.6%	13%

b.   This level of operation is most profitable for the Bottle Division relative to sales. The Bottle Division's return on sales is more than three times the return on sales realized in the Perfume Division.

c.   The Bottle Division once existed as a separate company. As such it was purchased with a management control system intact. It may be assumed that it was left as a separate division for managerial control purposes--to be able to separately evaluate the performance of bottling from perfume production. However, the big question is whether any purpose is served in leaving the Bottle Division as a profit centre. It would seem that many of the conflicts between the Bottle and Perfume Divisions could be eliminated if the Bottle Division were made a cost centre. This would be appropriate since the Bottle Division has no outside sales; and hence, is accountable for none of the company's revenues.

(CMA adapted)

Problem 11

a.   One of the purposes of this problem is to demonstrate that the price that generates a 20% return on sales is sensitive to assumptions made about sales volume. At the existing volume (70% of capacity) fixed costs amount to $100 per unit. If this is the assumed level of operations for the coming year, the per-unit sales price that generates net income before taxes equal to 20% of sales would be:

Let S = Sales price per unit

$S - \$290 = 0.2S$

$0.8S = \$290$

$S = \underline{\$362.50}$

However, students may come up with alternative answers depending on the assumptions made with regard to volume. As volume rises, fixed costs per unit decline and the sales price required to generate a 20% return declines.

b.   As a practical matter, the highest possible price would be $260 per unit. This is the outside price and represents the cost that Conveyor Systems Division could acquire the pumps from an alternative supply source. Even though this price fails to meet the net income objectives of the Hydraulic Division, any higher price will cause the division to lose the internal business.

c.   The division should charge any price that will cause the Conveyor Systems Division to purchase internally. The company's variable cost to produce the pump is $120 + $40 + $30 = $190. Since the market price is $260, the company is $70 per unit better off if the pump is made rather than purchased. The actual transfer price is irrelevant to the determination of overall corporate profits; however, the transfer price will affect the relative profits of the buying and selling divisions. From the company's perspective, any transfer price that causes the Conveyor Systems Division to purchase internally is optimal. Thus, the likely range of prices is $190 to $260.

(CMA adapted)

CHAPTER 11
MEASURING AND REWARDING PERFORMANCE

QUESTIONS

1.   The measurement system should
  - assess progress toward achievement of organizational goals and objectives;
  - be based on the input of those being evaluated;
  - consider the skills, information and authority of those being evaluated; and
  - provide necessary feedback in a timely and useful manner to managers.

3.   Because managerial pay is linked to their performance, managers will take actions to maximize their *measured* performance. This is why selection of performance measures is so important; if the wrong measures are selected, managers will attempt to maximize less important dimensions of performance. The selected measures should be the ones that are most highly correlated with the organization's goals and objectives.

5.   The major difference between a profit and an investment centre is that the investment centre has control over costs, revenues and the level of assets employed. Accordingly, investment centres need to be evaluated based on their profitability relative to the value of assets used. Profit centres have no responsibility for assets and can be evaluated based on profit alone.

7   Residual income, RI, is a derivative of return on investment, ROI. In many respects the relationship between ROI and RI is parallel to the relationship between net present value, NPV, and internal rate of return, IRR (Chapter 8). RI provides a dollar measure of divisional achievement while ROI provides a percentage measure of achievement. The principal strength of RI is that it creates fewer problems with suboptimization than ROI. In particular, RI minimizes the suboptimization problems associated with ROI when ROI varies substantially across a company's divisions.

9.   Conceptually, economic value added, EVA, is a measure of profits less the cost of capital. It is computed by subtracting a target rate of return, multiplied by the level of invested capital, from after-tax income.

   EVA is conceptually superior to residual income because invested capital is a better measure of investment than is the book value or market value of assets. Also, EVA is based on an after-tax profit measure rather than a pretax profit measure. It is only the after-tax profits that accrue to the benefit of investors in common stock.

11.   Throughput is the number of good units produced and sold during a given period of time. Throughput is based on number of units sold rather than units produced because no revenue or profit is generated by producing units that are not currently in demand by customers. Thus, goods only create value for the firm when they are sold, not when they are produced.

13.   Activity-based costing provides managers with a tool for looking at activities through the eyes of their customers. Customers want to pay only for activities that add value for them. ABC helps managers identify non-value-adding activities and provides a natural mechanism for relating activities to cost control. Thus, ABC provides a natural link between customer value and organizational activities and, further, it provides the measures necessary to evaluate progress in reducing costs and increasing customer value.

15.   Linking the compensation system to the performance evaluation system provides the incentive for managers to be concerned about the performance measures. The linkage makes the maximization of the performance measures the objective of the manager. If correct measures are identified, maximization of the performance measures should result in the achievement of the organization's goals and objectives.

17.   Maintaining a fair and equitable compensation system is more difficult for global operations. Some of the additional variables that must be considered are: the cost of living, safety considerations or other personal risk factors, differing tax laws across countries, fluctuations in foreign exchange rates, compensation paid by competitors, and cultural differences between countries.

EXERCISES

Exercise 1
a.   10
b.   5
c.   4
d.   6
e.   9
f.   1
g.   3
h.   2
i.   7
j.   8

Exercise 3
a.   ($14,400,000 - $13,004,000) ÷ $14,400,000 = <u>9.70%</u>

b. $14,400,000 ÷ $3,600,000 = 4

c.   9.70% x 4 = <u>38.8%</u>   ← *wrong answer?*

Exercise 5
a.   Segment Margin = Average Assets x ROI
      Segment Margin = $3,400,000 x 0.125 = <u>$425,000</u>

b.   Total Revenues = Segment Margin + Direct Expenses
      Total Revenues = $425,000 + $1,275,000 = <u>$1,700,000</u>

c.   Asset Turnover = Total Revenues ÷ Average Assets
      Asset Turnover = $1,700,000 ÷ $3,400,000 = <u>0.50</u>

d.   Profit Margin = Segment Margin ÷ Total Revenues
      Profit Margin = $425,000 ÷ $1,700,000 = <u>25%</u>

e.   ROI = Asset Turnover x Profit Margin
      ROI = .50 x 25% = <u>12.5%</u>

Exercise 7
a.   North Division: $30,000 - ($180,000 x .12) = <u>$ 8,400</u>
      South Division: $68,000 - ($290,000 x .12) = <u>$33,200</u>

b.   Based on the residual income criterion, the South Division is more successful.

Exercise 9
EVA = After-tax Income - (Cost of Capital x Invested Capital)
EVA = $1,800,000 - (.16 x $12,000,000)
EVA = $1,800,000 - $1,920,000 = <u>$(120,000)</u>

Exercise 11
a.   **EVA by Year:**
            Year 1: $800,000 - ($8,000,000 x 0.13) = $(240,000)
            Year 2: $800,000 - ($8,000,000 x 0.13) = $(240,000)
            Year 3: $1,160,000 - ($8,000,000 x 0.13) = $ 120,000
            Year 4: $2,900,000 - ($8,000,000 x 0.13) = $1,860,000
            Year 5: $2,700,000 - ($8,000,000 x 0.13) = $1,660,000

b.   **Compensation by Year:**
            Year 1: $(240,000) x 0.12 = $(28,800)
            Year 2: $(240,000) x 0.12 = $(28,800)
            Year 3: $ 120,000 x 0.12 = $14,400
            Year 4: $1,860,000 x 0.12 = $223,200
            Year 5: $1,660,000 x 0.12 = $199,200

c.   Whether Ms. Jenks will be hesitant to invest or not depends largely on her
      personal time horizon. Although investing in the project would reduce her
      compensation during the first three years, this reduction would be more than
      offset in the last two years. If Ms. Jenks' time horizon is three years or less, she
      is unlikely to invest. If her time horizon is four years or more, she is likely to
      invest. Also, Ms. Jenks must deal with the possibility that she would be dismissed
      from her position in one of the first three years due to poor performance if she
      invests in the project.

d.   Yes. Upper management would likely view the project favourably. The project
      appears to generate a return far in excess of the cost of capital after Year 2.

e.   Some measures that could be adopted include growth in market share, growth in
      sales, number of new customers served, rate of customer retention, and
      customer satisfaction rates.

Exercise 13

	Performance		**Explanation**
a.	Q	-	This measure captures the quality of production processes.
b.	CS	-	Percent on-time shipments measures how frequently customers are receiving their goods when they were promised receipt.
c.	RM or F	-	Manufacturing cycle time captures the extent to which a firm is using its available capacity.
d.	Q	-	This measure captures the percentage of units started that are completed and nondefective.
e.	Q	-	This is a measure of process quality.
f.	RM	-	Output per labour dollar measures the efficiency of utilizing direct labour.
g.	Q or CS	-	Number of crisis calls measures the rate of product failure.
h.	F	-	Changeover time measures how flexible production systems are in changing from the production of one product to another.
i.	RM	-	Machine downtime represents wasted productive capacity.
j.	Q	-	Supplier rejects measures the quality of product design and production processes for incoming components and materials.

Exercise 15
a. Has no effect on turnover.
b. Decreases the turnover ratio relative to what it could be if the unused assets were sold.
c. Decreases the turnover ratio relative to what it would be if the obsolete inventory were sold.
d. Decreases the turnover ratio.
e. Increases the turnover ratio.
f. Has no effect on the turnover ratio.

Exercise 17 Student answers may include any five of the following:
a. Cost-volume-profit (CVP) analysis should be carried out on each of the products of the firm to identify those products that have high contribution margins per unit and could benefit from increased marketing/promotion efforts. On the other hand, those products with low contribution margins per unit may be realizing reduced benefit from marketing/promotion efforts. CVP will provide management with insights into the effectiveness of their marketing efforts.

b. Use ROI and RI to evaluate the performance of the decentralized divisions. ROI/RI will encourage managers of the divisions to perform in ways that improve the performance of the entire organization.

c.   Use the budget as a means of making managers more accountable. Effective budgeting will enable the division managers to budget and control their expenditure more. It will also increase the goal clarity and the goal congruent behaviours of managers. This increased focus will likely improve the efficiency of the firm.

d.   Identify the critical success factors of each division and ensure that those attributes are measured and managers are evaluated relative to these factors. When managers become aware of the measures used to evaluate their performance, they will endeavour to perform well on those attributes. This could result in increased performance for the firm as a whole.

e.   Consider using segment reporting. Segment reporting will quickly identify those segments that are less/more profitable and thereby provide insights into where problems and opportunities are present.

f.   Consider using just-in-time (JIT) inventory management. JIT reduces inventory carrying costs, which, for most manufacturing firms, could be significant.

g.   Encourage a total quality management (TQM) attitude. With a TQM mentality, the firm is more likely to be successful in a competitive environment. This will result in improved sales and profits.

Extract from *Management Accounting Examinations* published by the Certified General Accountants Association of Canada (© CGA-Canada 1999). Reprinted with permission.

PROBLEMS

Problem 1

a.

	Actual Amounts	**Flexible Budget**	**Master Budget**	
Sales	$13,000,000	$13,000,000	$12,000,000	100%
Variable costs	9,750,000	9,100,000	8,400,000	70%
CM	$ 3,250,000	$ 3,900,000	$3,600,000	30%
Fixed costs	2,410,000	2,400,000	2,400,000	
Pretax income	$ 840,000	$ 1,500,000	$ 1,200,000	

The data show that the actual pretax income fell short of the expected amount by $360,000 ($1,200,000 - $840,000). This occurred despite the fact that the actual level of sales exceeded the expected level by $1,000,000. The higher level of sales would have generated an additional $300,000 of income ($1,500,000 - $1,200,000) if costs and prices would have been maintained at the budgeted level. However, this effect was overwhelmed by either a lower per-unit sales price or a higher per-unit variable cost. The budgeted contribution margin was to be 30 percent of sales. The actual contribution margin was only 25 percent of sales ($3,250,000) $13,000,000). Without knowing the number of units that were sold, the price and variable cost effects cannot be disentangled. By having the actual CM drop by 5 percent, pretax profits were lowered by $650,000 ($3,900,000 - $3,250,000). This is the principal cause of the drop in profits. A more minor effect was the increase in fixed costs. These exceeded the budgeted level by $10,000. These differences can be summarized as follows:

Effect of increase in volume	$ 300,000
Effect of decrease in CM%	(650,000)
Effect of increase in fixed costs	(10,000)
Net effect on pretax income	$(360,000)

b. Complete income statements provide more information for isolating the cause of differences between the budgeted and expected levels of income. By comparing only the actual and budgeted levels of pretax income, nothing is learned about the cause of the difference.

c. The nonfinancial measures should be designed to capture organizational efficiency. For general efficiency, throughput could be used along with its component ratios and other measures such as percent good output, output per labour dollar, and first-time-through rejection rates; for control of quality costs, statistics could be gathered for costs of scrap, waste, and rework; for period costs, a ratio of period costs to sales would be useful, as would a ratio of selling costs per customer served. Many other measures could be developed once areas of operational inefficiency are identified.

Problem 3

a. Calculate net income:

	Johnson	First Star	Nolan Bay
Revenues	$12,600,000	$16,200,000	$14,400,000
Expenses	11,340,000	15,228,000	12,420,000
Segment Margin	$ 1,260,000	$ 972,000	$ 1,980,000

Calculate profit margin:

	Johnson	First Star	Nolan Bay
Segment Margin	$ 1,260,000	$ 972,000	$ 1,980,000
Divide by Revenues	$12,600,000	$16,200,000	$14,400,000
Profit Margin	10%	6%	13.75%

Calculate asset turnover:

	Johnson	First Star	Nolan Bay
Revenues	$12,600,000	$16,200,000	$14,400,000
Divide by assets	$ 6,300,000	$ 5,400,000	$ 7,200,000
Asset turnover	2	3	2

ROI = profit margin x asset turnover

=	10% x 2	6% x 3	13.75% x 2
=	20%	18%	27.5%

b. According to the ROI calculations, Nolan Bay appears to be the strongest company and First Star appears to be the weakest. Given only this information, Nolan Bay would be the best investment because it is returning more profit per dollar of assets.

c. While First Star has the lowest ROI, it has the highest asset turnover ratio. Unfortunately, its low profit margin appears to be dominating its high asset turnover and the consequence is a low ROI. This suggests First Star could improve its ROI by either lowering expenses or raising prices. In either case, profitability per dollar of sales would improve. Even if the asset turnover ratio declines slightly, the ROI would likely improve. Note that the two companies with the higher ROIs have an asset turnover ratio of only 2.

Problem 5

a. 1. $400,000 ÷ $2,000,000 = 20%
    2. $2,000,000 ÷ $4,000,000 = 0.5
    3. $400,000 ÷ 0.10 = $4,000,000
    4. $16,000,000 x 0.15 = $2,400,000
    5. $16,000,000 ÷ 1.4 = $11,428,571 (rounded)
    6. 1.4 x 15% = 21%
    7. $1,000,000 ÷ $8,000,000 = 12.5%
    8. $8,000,000 ÷ $4,000,000 = 2
    9. $1,000,000 ÷ $4,000,000 = 25%

b.   Overall, the Storage Division posted the strongest performance as measured by ROI. While it had the lowest profit margin, it had the highest asset turnover ratio. The Transport Division placed in the middle on all three performance measures. The Package Division managed to generate the highest profit margin, but its investment in assets was too high for the achieved level of sales. This resulted in a very poor asset turnover ratio and the lowest ROI of the three divisions.

Problem 7

	Asset turnover	**Profit margin**	**ROI**	**RI**
a.	IN	D	D	D*
b.	IN	D	IN	IN
c.	IN	IN	IN	IN
d.	N	IN	IN	IN
e.	N	N	N	D
f.	D	IN	I	I
g.	IN	I	I	I
h.	D	IN	I	I

*As long as the return < 100% of average assets.

Thus, according to the projections, the project under evaluation by the manager of Pleasure Division would cause his/her overall residual income to decline by an amount equal to 3 percent of the cost of the investment. On the other hand, the project under consideration by the manager of Commercial Division would generate an overall increase in RI equal to 1 percent of the cost of the new investment.

Problem 9

a.   Projected EVA = \$3,500,000 - (\$25,000,000 x 0.12) = <u>\$500,000</u>

b.   You would not invest in the project if it would result in a decline in your overall projected EVA. Therefore, the maximum amount that you would invest would be the amount that would leave your projected EVA unchanged:

         Pretax additional earnings   \$400,000
         Taxes (\$400,000 x 0.30)   <u>(120,000)</u>
         After-tax change in earnings   <u>\$280,000</u>
         Maximum investment x 0.12 = \$280,000
         Maximum investment = \$280,000 ÷ 0.12
         Maximum investment = <u>\$2,333,333</u>

c.   After-tax income = \$3,500,000 + \$280,000 = \$3,780,000

     Invested capital = \$25,000,000 + \$1,100,000
                   = \$26,100,000

     EVA = \$3,780,000 - (\$26,100,000 x 0.12) = <u>\$648,000</u>

Problem 11

a.   2006 ROI: $\dfrac{\$360{,}000}{\$1{,}800{,}000}$ = 20%

     2007 ROI: $\dfrac{\$735{,}000}{\$4{,}000{,}000}$ = 18.375%

b.   2006 RI = $360,000 - ($1,800,000 x 0.16) = $72,000
     2007 RI = $735,000 - ($4,000,000 x 0.16) = $95,000

     My performance would be better since I have an RI of $95,000 compared to $72,000 of the previous manager.

c.   The ROI of 18.375% in 2007 is lower because of a large increase in the denominator (average assets employed). This came about because of the need to replace the obsolete plant and equipment and that which had been sold at the end of 2006 by the previous division manager. The disposal of assets at the end of 2006 increased the ROI measure since the average assets employed would have decreased by the amount disposed of. This action could be detrimental to the long-run interests of Fruta. My effort to overcome this action by the previous manager results in a lower ROI in 2007. However, the RI in 2007 is higher than in 2006, which implies that the incremental contribution to Fruta is higher in 2007 and that operating net income in 2007 was high enough to cover the larger cost of capital.

d.   Given that the ROI on that project was only 18% ($90,000/$500,000), it is not surprising that the previous manager did not undertake this project. If he had taken it on, his ROI would have been lower than his 2006 ROI of 20%. It would have reduced his ROI to 19.6% [($360,000+ $90,000)/($1,800,000 + $500,000)].

e.   The CEO seemed to be comparing my RI of $95,000 with the RI of one of my competitors of $1,000,000 [$5,000,000 - ($25,000,000 x 0.16)]. This demonstrates one of the disadvantages of the RI measure. Based on the size of assets, this competitor is more than 6 times as large as Fruta. Because of the larger asset base, the RI will tend to be higher than that of a smaller firm. The lack of comparability across firms with different sizes is one of the major disadvantages of using RI. A comparison will be more meaningful if made with a firm of approximately the same size as Fruta.

CHAPTER 12
COST MANAGEMENT AND PERFORMANCE
MEASUREMENT SYSTEMS

QUESTIONS

1. A cost management system may be very useful in strategic and management decisions. To illustrate, a sophisticated CMS will be able to provide useful life-cycle cost information. The life-cycle cost information will allow managers to evaluate trade-offs in costs over the life cycle of a product. To reduce production costs associated with poor design or poor quality, managers may elect to invest heavily in research and development to improve the product's design and production process. By providing information on life-cycle costs under a variety of assumptions about the product and process design, the CMS contributes substantially to a firm's strategic and management decisions.

3   *Financial accounting:* information about valuation of inventories, other assets, and cost of goods sold.
    Production reporting: measurement of product cost and production volume, cost of labour, cost of overhead and materials consumed.
    Inventory management: cost of carrying inventory, cost of making inventory, cost of inventory outages.
    Production planning and scheduling: historical information regarding product demand, projections on future product demand, setup costs, inventory storage costs, economic order quantity.
    Research and development: estimation of R&D cost, estimation of expected benefits from R&D activities, product life cycle information, tax benefits of R&D.
    Quality control: cost of quality assessment, cost of quality failure (internal and external), rate of quality defects, various measurements of achieved quality.
    Marketing: costs of alternative product promotion strategies; information regarding product distribution costs; product sales information by area, product, salesperson; life cycle product costs, profitability measurements.

5. Managers might be willing to accept errors or miscalculations in information if the cost of getting more accurate information were too high or if the time required to obtain more accurate information were too long. Timeliness and cost are two important factors that managers must consider in determining when to acquire more accurate information.

7. Separate control systems are necessary because no single control system can be effective for all dimensions of performance. For example, firms have activities related to purchasing, selling, operating, hiring, and contracting. All of these and other areas will require control systems.

9.   Cost management systems are not sufficient. Knowing the costs is important and necessary, but managers and operators need to know on an ongoing basis – hourly or at least daily – the effectiveness and efficiency of the performance of activities.

11.   The four stages are:
      ▪ Stage I: inadequate for financial report. Crude systems that produce inaccurate product/service cost information.
      ▪ Stage II: financial reporting driven. Accurate financial reporting, but as financial reporting dominates, products/services cost accuracy is subservient to financial reporting standards.
      ▪ Stage III: customized, managerially relevant, stand-alone. Separate systems exist for product/service costing, financial reporting, and performance measurement.
      ▪ Stage IV: integrated cost management, financial reporting, and performance. Integrated or ERP system where product/service costing, financial reporting, and performance measurement are a single system based on activities.

13.   Some ERP brands include: SAP, PeopleSoft, and Oracle.

15.   The three basic approaches for ERP business process redesign:

      ▪ First, change all processes to achieve the ideal set of business processes. With these changes, there may be difficulties with implementing an ERP system as the new processes may be inconsistent with ERP system requirements.
      ▪ Second, accept the ERP design. This allows for fast implementation – and the saving of time, human energy, and money–because issues regarding process redesign are avoided. Generally, with this approach the disadvantage is the lack of flexibility; business processes that use the ERP vendor's design might not be sufficiently appropriate for the organization.
      ▪ Third, redesign with the ERP system in mind. This approach is often called "ERP design by default." The advantage of this approach is that for most processes the plain ERP system is adequate. For those few cases where customized software is crucial, the extra cost needs to be incurred.

17.   Wal-Mart's Retail Link is an ERP system plus a supply chain management (SCM) system, which integrates its electronic data interchange (EDI) network with an extranet used by Wal-Mart buyers and some 10,000 suppliers to gather and disseminate information about sales and inventory levels in every store.

19. In designing the organizational structure, top managers normally will try to group subunits either geographically or by similar missions or natural product clusters. These aggregation processes provide effective cost management because of proximity or similarity of units under a single manager's control.

21. They are equally important. They are all integral to the design of effective cost management and performance measurement systems. Only if all three elements are designed properly will cost management and performance measurement systems serve to effectively and efficiently implement the organization's strategies.

23. Gap analysis is the formal comparison of the ideal cost management system of a specific firm to its existing cost management system. Gap analysis is used to update cost management systems by bringing focus to the differences between the existing system and an ideal system. These differences or "gaps" are the areas in which managers strive to make improvements.

25. Large, complex organizations implement ERP systems.

EXERCISES

Exercise 1
a   9
b   7
c   4
d   6
e   8
f   10
g   1
h   3
i   2
j   5

Exercise 3
a   BPR
b   PRE
c   PRE
d   PRE
e   PRE
f   PRE
g   BPR
h   PRE
i   BPR

Exercise 5
The answer will depend upon the selected organization

Exercise 7
For a Deli, important performance information would include: number of customers per hour, number of customers served per employee per hour, dollar sales per hour, dollar sales per hour per employee, sales mix, customer satisfaction.

Exercise 9
Stage II organizations are able to meet financial reporting requirements and to collect costs accurately by responsibility centres (but not by activities and business processes). In other words, they are adequate for valuing inventory for financial reporting purposes and for preparing periodic financial reports. However, these systems produce highly distorted product costs because traditional allocations systems are used instead of ABC (see Chapter 6 for a discussion), and relatedly they have nonexistent or highly distorted customer costs and performance feedback that is too late, too aggregated, and too financial.

Stage II systems are able to prepare complete financial statements shortly after the end of an accounting period that require minimal postclosing adjustments. Product or service costing with Stage II systems report individual product or service costs with the same simple and aggregate methods used for external financial reporting, to value inventory, and to measure cost of goods sold. The problems with Stage II are:

- the inability to estimate the cost of activities and business processes, and therefore the cost and profitability of products, services, and customers, and
- the inability to provide useful feedback to improve business processes.

These deficiencies are a result of the financial reporting system that is being used for both product costing and performance measurement. Financial reporting systems, although appropriate for external reporting, do not operate at the activity level which is necessary for accurate costing and performance measurement. Consequently, Stage II systems do not provide adequate information to managers for planning, decision making, and control.

Exercise 11
Stage IV systems have ABC and performance measurement systems that are integrated and together provide the basis for preparing external financial reporting. Consequently no fundamental conflict exists between the product costs from the ABC system and the external requirements for financial reporting. The ABC cost drivers are used for assigning overhead costs for both internal decision making and external financial reporting. Any allocations – i.e., nonmanufacturing costs – that do not comply with GAAP, regulatory requirements, or tax rules – can be eliminated for external financial reporting. Simple attribute fields for activities can identify these noninventoriable costs for the system to eliminate them from product costs in inventory accounts. The same information is provided by both Stage III and Stage IV systems, but the Stage IV system will be more accurate because of the integration of systems and data, i.e.,

- a traditional but well-functioning financial reporting system capable of basic accounting and transaction-capturing functions, such as preparing monthly and quarterly financial statements for external stakeholders. This information would be produced monthly.
- one or more activity-based costing systems that use data from the financial reporting and other systems to measure the cost of organizational units, customers, products, services, processes, and activities. This information would be produced periodically as needed.
- performance measurement systems of various types that provide front line workers and their superiors with timely, accurate information – financial and nonfinancial – on the efficiency and effectiveness of activities and processes. This information would be produced daily or more frequently.

Exercise 13

A chart of accounts is the codes that identify physical activities in an organization, as well as assets, liabilities, revenues, and expenses, for accurate recording, for cost management, financial reporting, and performance measurement. The chart of accounts converts all relevant activities into a numerical hierarchical system that is easy to manipulate for producing information for decision making. A chart of accounts is important with ERP systems as it allows intra- and inter-organizational parts to be pulled or brought together through the common data warehouse. Through these standardized processes, activities and information, all parts can be managed in comparable terms.

Exercise 15

Critical success factors for Wal-Mart include: wide selection of products, lowest possible prices, all aspects of the organization linked together with low cost information. Critical success factors for Dell include: customized product/made to order, all aspects of the organization linked together with low cost information, supplier and customer facing systems.

Exercise 17

Performance measurement information relevant to a driver testing centre would include: number of appointments per day, number of appointments per driving examiner, percent of appointments kept, number of administrative staff per driving examiner, average cost per driving test, and average fee per driving test.

WEB CHAPTER 13
CAPITAL ASSET SELECTION AND CAPITAL BUDGETING

QUESTIONS

1.   A capital asset is an asset that provides benefits to the firm for more than one year. Capital assets are primarily distinguished from other assets in that they have longer lives, and they exist only to provide the capacity for the firm to produce, distribute and market goods.

3.   The screening evaluation is used only to determine if a project meets some predetermined standard (net present value > 0, for example). In simply meeting this criterion, the project is not necessarily going to be funded. To be funded, a project must be evaluated based on how it compares to other projects that have also passed the screening criterion. This comparison will involve preference criteria. The preference criteria may take into account nonfinancial data: safety considerations, legal requirements, public service obligations, etc. Also, the preference criteria will need to take into account that some projects are mutually exclusive, others are mutually inclusive, and yet others are independent.

4.   The purpose of discounted cash flow analysis is to account for the opportunity cost of money for transactions that occur at different points in time. There is no opportunity cost associated with accounting accruals, only cash transactions. Accordingly, discounted cash flow analysis focuses only on those transactions in which an opportunity cost (interest) exists

7.   The payback period is the amount of time required for cash inflows to recoup the initial cost of an investment. Usually, no allowance is made for the time value of money in computing the payback period. This is one reason it is normally used only in conjunction with other methods. Another reason is that the payback method ignores all cash flows that occur after the payback period.

9.   If the NPV = 0, then the projected return on the project is equal to the discount rate. If the NPV < 0, the project's expected return is below the firm's discount rate; and if the NPV > 0, the expected return exceeds the firm's discount rate.

11. The profitability index, PI, is a measure that provides more information about relative "profitability" of two projects that are of dissimilar size. The PI relates the present value of each project to its initial cost. The net present value measure provides no indication of the actual cost of each investment.

13. Unique to the IRR, two major weaknesses are: (1) the IRR ignores the dollar magnitude of alternative projects, and (2) projects with large cash outflows in the later years of their lives may generate multiple IRRs.

14.   A profitability index is the present value of the net cash flows from an investment divided by its cost. The index provides the relative measurement needed to compare two or more investments of different sizes to ensure that a firm uses its limited resources for investments with the largest returns

16.   A net present value of zero does not mean that a firm earns zero profit from the investments. It simply means that the return was equal to the firm's cost of capital thus value was not added.

18.   Like other capital projects, environmental projects often involve a cash outlay in the present period that is expected to generate benefits over several future periods. Thus, capital budgeting techniques are appropriate for the evaluation of such projects.

21.*   The accounting rate of return is the only method which relies on accrual-based accounting information rather than cash flows. Net income is determined by both cash flows and noncash expenses and revenues. For example, depreciation is a noncash expense, and the gain recognized on the sale of an asset is a noncash revenue.

23.*   CCA reduces the amount of taxes which are payable. Depreciation is used for book purposes but CCA (Capital Cost Allowance) is used to calculate the expense for the use of capital asset. The impact of this is to reduce the amount of cash outlay for taxes.

*Appendix

EXERCISES

Exercise 1

a.   Payback = $120,000) $40,000 = <u>3</u> years for both projects

Based on the payback criterion, the projects are equally desirable.

b.   The projects are not equally desirable, even though they have the same payback. Project B's life is a full year longer than project A's life. Thus, the sum of cash flows to be derived from Project B exceeds the sum from Project A. This indicates a need to use a secondary method to evaluate capital projects when the payback method is used.

Exercise 3

Time:	t0	t1	t2	t3	t4	t5
Amount	$(300,000)	$125,000	$125,000	$40,000	$40,000	$40,000

Cash flow Description	Time	Amount	Discount Factor	Present Value
Purchase machine	t0	$(300,000)	1.0000	$(300,000)
Cash inflow	t1	125,000	0.9091	113,638
Cash inflow	t2	125,000	0.8265	103,313
Cash inflow	t3	40,000	0.7513	30,052
Cash inflow	t4	40,000	0.6830	27,320
Cash inflow	t5	40,000	0.6209	24,836
NPV				$ (841)

Exercise 7

a.   Present value of cash inflows = $630,000 x 4.3553 = $2,743,839
this is the maximum that the firm could pay and still have a non-negative NPV.

b. $2,743,839 ÷ $630,000 = <u>4.36</u> years (rounded)

c.   The marketing manager might question the following: how sales of the licensed product would affect sales of other products, how sales would be affected

at the end of the license agreement if the agreement is not renewed, how competitors might respond to the license agreement, and whether the estimates of sales of the licensed product are reasonable.

Exercise 10

a.   PV of inflows = $12,000 x 4.1114 = $49,337
      PI = $49,337. $55,475 = 0.89

b.   Discount factor of IRR = $55,475. $12,000 = 4.6229
      IRR (4.6229, 6 years) = 8%

      No, this is not an acceptable investment. Since the project has an internal
      rate of return of 8%, and a PI less than 1, it would have a negative NPV if
      12% were used as the discount rate

Exercise 13

The written report should emphasize that the future revenues of firms are determined, in
part, by actions taken in the present to develop new products and services. The
development process is controlled by research and development programs which, in turn,
are controlled by the capital budget.

By developing a rigorous capital budgeting system, potential research and development
projects would be critically examined and approved only if they met stated performance
criteria. The performance criteria would include financial measures such as net present
value or internal rate of return. By establishing the financial criteria at high levels, only the
most profitable research and development projects, and those with the greatest likelihood
of success, would be approved.

*Exercise 15

Cost = $6,000 + $400 × annuity discount factor (48 periods, 1%)
$6,000 + ($400 × 37.974) = $21,190

*Exercise 17

a.
Cash flow			**Discount**	**Present**
Description	**Time**	**Amount**	**Factor**	**Value**
Purchase blender	t0	$(300,000)	1.0000	$(300,000)
Cost savings	t1-t10	50,000	6.1446	307,230
NPV				$ 7,230

b. $307,230) $300,000 = 1.02 (rounded)

c. $50,000 × discount factor = $300,000
      discount factor = 6.000(10-year annuity)
      IRR = approximately 10.5%

d. $300,000 ÷ $50,000 = 6 years

e.   Average annual income = $50,000 - ($300,000 ÷ 10) = $20,000
      ARR = $20,000 ÷ ($300,000 ÷ 2) = <u>13.33</u>%

*Exercise 20

a.   Cash flows associated with the machine replacement decision for next year.

	Old Machine	New Machine
Selling price per unit [$140 x (1 - 0.10)]	$ 126.00	$ 126.00
Less: Variable costs per unit[1]		
Direct materials	28.00	28.00
Direct labour		
3 hours x ($12 x 1.05)	37.80	
2.8 hours x ($12 x 1.05)		35.28
Variable overhead		
3 hours x $4/hour	12.00	
2.8 hours x $4/hour		11.20
Contribution margin per unit	$ 48.20	$ 51.52
Number of units	55,000	55,000
Total contribution margin	<u>$2,651,000</u>	<u>$2,833,600</u>

[1] Fixed overhead costs are not relevant to the decision. They would be the same regardless of which machine is used.

b.   Net present value:

Item	Year(s)	Amount	Tax Effect	After-Tax Cash Flow	14% Interest Factor	PV of Cash Flow
(1) Cost of new machine	0	$(1,000,000)	–	$(1,000,000)	1.0000	$(1,000,000)
(1) Market value of old machine	0	375,000	–	375,000	1.000	375,000

(3) Annual contribution margin cash flows	1–5	182,600[1]	(1–0.4)	109,560	3.4331	376,130
(3) PV of salvage value of new machine	5	425,000	–	425,000	0.5194	220,745
(3) PV of CCA tax shield[2]						138,029
(3) PV of lost CCA tax shield on salvage value[3]						(51,937)
Net present value						$57,967

[1] Relevant cash flows for the decision = $2,833,600 - $2,651,000 = $182,600

[2] $$\frac{[(\$1,000,000 - \$375,000) \times (0.20 \times 0.40)]}{(0.20 + 0.14)} \times \frac{[1+ (0.5 \times 0.14)]}{1 + 0.14} = \$138,029$$

[3] $$\frac{[\$425,000 \times (0.20 \times 0.40)]}{(0.20 + 0.14)} \times \frac{1}{(1 + 0.14)^5} = \$51,937$$

Conclusion: The Company should replace the old machine because the net present value is positive.

PROBLEMS

Problem 1

a.

Year	Cash flow	PV factor	PV
0	$(2,500,000)	1.0000	$(2,500,000)
1-7	409,000[1]	5.0330	2,058,497
7	200,000	0.5470	109,400
NPV			$ (332,103)

[1] $409,000 = $465,000 - $20,000 - $14,000 - $22,000

b.   No, the NPV is negative; therefore this is an unacceptable project.

c.   PI = NPV of future cash flows) present value of investment
        = ($2,058,497 + $109,400)) $2,500,000 = 0.87

d.   The company should consider the quality of the work performed by the machine versus the quality of the work performed by the individuals; the reliability of the manual process versus the reliability of the mechanical process; and perhaps most importantly, the effect on worker morale and the ethical considerations in displacing 14 workers.

e.   The conveyor system could have a positive impact on quality. One way to impound quality considerations in the analysis is to estimate the reduction in annual quality costs that would result from the investment. If the company has a quality-sensitive chart of accounts, the amount of costs to be saved by investing in the new system should be calculable. After considering these costs in the discounted cash flow analysis, the project may generate an acceptable NPV.

Problem 2

a.   Net cash flow = $220,00 - $22,000 - $14,000 - $14,000 = $170,000

Cash flow Description	Time	Amount	Discount Factor	Present Value
Purchase machine	t0	($1,200,000)	1.0000	($1,200,000)
Net annual cash flow	t1-t10	170,000	5.2161	886,737
Salvage value	t10	100,000	0.2697	26,970
Net present value				($ 286,293)

b.   Because the NPV < 0, the company should not buy the machine.

c.   The company should carefully consider whether it has accounted for all effects of the new technology: product quality, production capacity, worker impact, ability to adopt other new technologies in the future

Problem 10

a.   Annual cost savings from new technology:

Acid A: (40 - 10) × 750 × $2 $45,000
Acid B: (20 - 5) × 750 × $2   22,500
Total annual cost savings $ 67,500

NPV calculation

Cash flow Description	time	Amount	Discount Factor	Present Value
Buy equipment	t0	$(500,000)	1.0000	$(500,000)
Annual cash flow	t1-t6	67,500	4.4859	302,798
NPV				$(197,202)

Based on the NPV criterion, the project is unacceptable.

b.   Although the NPV indicates the project is unacceptable financially by a wide margin, there are other factors to be considered.

- By reducing the waste of acids A and B, the firm may not only save the disposal costs included in the calculation, but also the purchase costs of the quantity of each acid that is wasted under the existing technology.
- Disposal costs of the waste acids may rise to a level much higher than $2 in the future. It may be unreasonable to assume the costs will remain at this level.
- If the new technology reduces the quantity of acids to be purchased because of the reduction in waste, society may further benefit by a reduction in the quantity of harmful waste and by-products generated by Poë Chemical's suppliers of the acids.
- If the volume of the chemical solvent produced increases in the future, the amount of savings generated by the new technology would be greater than estimated assuming constant future demand.
- By reducing its level of waste, the company may avoid future fines, penalties, and legal judgments that may be enforceable in the present but result from the generation of these harmful materials. For example, if the firm that is responsible for disposing of these acids acts improperly and causes environmental damage, Poë Chemical could be held liable for any resulting cleanup costs.

Problem 12

a. $t0 = -\$180,000 + \$40,000 = -\$140,000$
     $t1 - t0 = \$63,000$

     $NPV = -\$140,000 + (\$63,000 \times 5.0188)$
         $= -\$140,000 + \$316,184$
         $= \$176,184$

b.   2 years + $\$14,000 \div \$63,000 = 2.222$ years

c. $\$87,500 \div (\$140,000 \div 2) = 125\%$

d.

Incremental revenue ($30,000 X 10 years)	$300,000
Labour cost savings ($5,000 X 10 years)	50,000
Savings in other cash costs ($28,000 X 10 years)	280,000
Less incremental cost	(140,000)
Incremental profit	$490,000

Because the incremental profit is greater than $0, the firm should buy the new equipment.

Problem 15
Note   CCA ≈ Depreciation

a.   Calculate the CCA:

<u>Capital Cost Allowance and Undepreciated Capital Cost Schedules</u>

	UCC	CCA at 30%
Year 1	$36,000	$5,400 (remember the half-year rule)
Year 2	$30,600	$9,180
Year 3	$21,420	$6,426
Year 4	$14,994	$4,498
End of Year 4	$10,496	

Compute the cash flows:

		Year 1	Year 2	Year 3	Year 4
i	Cash savings	$13,000	$13,000	$13,000	$13,000
ii	Cash operating costs	1,500	1,500	1,500	1,500
iii	Net cash flows from operations (i–ii)	$11,500	$11,500	$11,500	$11,500
iv	CCA	5,400	9,180	6,426	4,498
v	Taxable income (iii–iv)	$ 6,100	$ 2,320	$ 5,074	$ 7,002
vi	Taxes (at 40%)	2,440	928	2,030	2,801
vii	After-tax cash flows (iii–vi)	$ 9,060	$10,572	$ 9,470	$ 8,699

Note that because there is remaining UCC in the pool, there will still be tax benefits accruing from this computer system even after it is obsolete.

b. From the table below, we see the payback period is less than 4 years.

	After-tax cash flows	Cumulative cash flows
Year 1	$ 9,060	$ 9,060
Year 2	$10,572	$19,632
Year 3	$ 9,470	$29,102
Year 4	$ 8,699	$37,801

At the end of the third year, $6,898 ($36,000 − $29,102) is needed to recover the original $36,000 investment. If the $8,699 cash flow occurs evenly throughout the year, it should take 0.8 of a year ($6,898 / $8,699) of the fourth year to recover the rest of the original investment, giving a payback period of 3.8 years.

c. To determine the accounting rate of return, first calculate the net income for each of the four years.

		Year 1	Year 2	Year 3	Year 4	Average
v	Taxable Income (iii–iv)	$6,100	$2,320	$5,074	$7,002	
vi	Taxes (at 40%)	$2,440	$ 928	$2,030	$2,801	
vii	Net Income (v–vi)	$3,660	$1,392	$3,044	$4,201	$3,074

Average investment is $18,000 = $36,000 ÷ 2
ARR = $3,074 ÷ $18,000 = 17.08%

Problem 18

a.   The PV of the cash flows:

		Year 1	Year 2	Year 3	Year 4	Year 5	Total
i.	Cash flows	$250,000	$500,000	$650,000	$2,000,000	$1,800,000	
ii.	Taxes (at 50%)	125,000	250,000	325,000	1,000,000	900,000	
iii.	After-tax cash flows	125,000	250,000	325,000	1,000,000	900,000	
iv.	Discount factor at (10%)	0.9091	0.8265	0.7513	0.6830	0.6209	
v.	PV of after-tax cash flows (iv*iii)	$113,638	$206,625	$244,173	$ 683,000	$ 558,810	$1,806,246

PV of CCA = ($2,500,000 × 0.3 × 0.5) ÷ (0.3 + 0.1) × [1 + (0.5 × 0.1) ÷ (1 + 0.1)] = $894,886

Since there is no salvage value,

NPV = - $2,500,000 + $1,806,246 + $894,886

      = $ 201,132

b.   Since the NPV is positive, Ms. Roberts will invest in the project. The project is profitable, on a pre-tax basis, in each of the five years. However, the total profits in years 1-3 are not enough to recover the initial investment. Therefore, if Ms. Roberts is evaluated only on the profits in those 3 years, she may decide not to proceed.

The project is profitable, on a pre-tax basis, in each of the five years. However, the total profits in years 1-3 are not enough to recover the initial investment. Therefore, if Ms. Roberts is evaluated only on the profits in those 3 years, she may decide not to proceed.

Problem 20

a. NPV = - initial investment + PV of after-tax cash flows + PV of CCA

= - $1,800,000 + $310,000 * (1 – 0.5) * 1/ k   {1 – 1/(1 + k) ^{15} }   + $1,800,000 * 0.2 * 0.5)] / 0.2 + k) * 1 + 0.5k / 1 = k

The IRR is the value of k that makes NPV = 0

Try 9%

(- $1,800,000 + $310,000) * (1 – 0.5) * 1 / 0.09   {1 - 1. /1,09) ^{15} } + { ($1,800,000 * 0.2 * 0.5 / 0.2 + 0.9) * (1.045 / 1.09)}

= - $1,800,000 + $1,249,409 + $595, 065

= $ 44,474

Try 10%

- $1,800,000 + { $310,000 * (1 – 0.5) * 1 / 0.10 {1 – 1/ (1.10) ^{15}} + {($1,800,000 * 0.2 * 0.5) / (0.2 + 0.10)} * (1.05 / 1.10)

= - $1,800,000 + $1,178,942 + $572,727

= - $48,330

The IRR is between 9% and 10%, closer to 9%

163

Alternative Solution

Try 9%
Step One: Present value of tax shield

PV [($1,800,000 x 0.2 x 0.5) ÷ (0.2 + 0.09)] x [(1 + 0.045) / (1 + 0.l09)]
= [($180,000 ÷ 0.29) x 0.9587]
= $595,055

Present Value of net annual savings:

[($310,000 x 0.5) x 8.0607] = $1,249,409

N.P.V. = - $1,800,000 + $595,055 + $1,249,409
       = $44,064

Try 10%
P.V. = [($1,800,000 x 0.2 x 0.5) ÷ (0.2 + 0.10)] x [1.05 ÷ 1.1]
     = ($180,000 ÷ 0.3) x 0.9545
     = $572,700

P.V. of annual savings = [$310,000 x (1 – 0.5)] x 7.6061
                       = $1,178,946

N.P.V. = -$1,800,000 + $1,178,946 + $572,700
       = -$48,354

b.   Some qualitative factors that might need to be considered are:
      - the competitive impact of not making the investment
      - health and safety issues and possible future regulatory considerations

c.　The table that follows shows the payback occurs during the eighth year.

Year	UCC i	CCA @ 20% ii	Cash savings iii	Taxable income (iii–ii) iv	Tax at 50% v	After-tax cash flows (iii–v) vi	Cumulative after-tax cash flows vii
1	$1,800,000	$180,000	$310,000	$130,000	$65,000	$245,000	$245,000
2	$1,620,000	$324,000	$310,000	$–14,000	$–7,000	$317,000	$562,000
3	$1,296,000	$259,200	$310,000	$ 50,800	$25,400	$284,600	$846,600
4	$1,036,800	$207,360	$310,000	$102,640	$51,320	$258,680	$1,105,280
5	$829,440	$165,888	$310,000	$144,112	$72,056	$237,944	$1,343,224
6	$663,552	$132,710	$310,000	$177,290	$88,645	$221,355	$1,564,579
7	$530,842	$106,168	$310,000	$203,832	$101,916	$208,084	$1,772,663
8	$424,673	$84,935	$ 310,000	$225,065	$112,533	$197,467	$1,970,130
9	$339,739	$67,948	$ 310,000	$242,052	$121,026	$188,974	$2,159,104
10	$271,791	$54,358	$ 310,000	$255,642	$127,821	$182,179	$2,341,283
11	$217,433	$43,487	$ 310,000	$266,513	$133,257	$176,743	$2,518,026
12	$173,946	$34,789	$ 310,000	$275,211	$137,606	$172,394	$2,690,420
13	$139,157	$27,831	$ 310,000	$282,169	$141,085	$168,915	$2,859,335
14	$111,326	$22,265	$ 310,000	$287,735	$143,868	$166,132	$3,025,467
15	$89,061	$17,812	$ 310,000	$292,188	$146,094	$163,906	$3,189,373

At the end of the seventh year, $27,337 ($1,800,000 – $1,772,663) is needed to recover the initial investment. If the cash flow occurs evenly throughout the eighth year, it should take 0.14 ($27,337) ÷ $197,467) of a year to recover the rest of the original $1,800,000 investment, giving a payback period of 7.14 years.